Striving Toward God

Spiritual Advice for Daily Living

Striving Toward God
Spiritual Advice for Daily Living

by Abbess Arsenia (Sebriakova)
[Anna Mikhailovna Sebriakova]

Translation, Introduction, and Biography
By Mary Naumenko

HOLY TRINITY PUBLICATIONS
The Printshop of St Job of Pochaev
Holy Trinity Monastery
Jordanville, New York
2016

Printed with the blessing of His Eminence,
Metropolitan Hilarion First Hierarch
of the Russian Orthodox Church Outside of Russia

Striving Toward God
Spiritual Advice for Daily Living

PRINTSHOP OF
SAINT JOB OF POCHAEV

An imprint of

HOLY TRINITY PUBLICATIONS
Holy Trinity Monastery
Jordanville, New York 13361-0036
www.holytrinitypublications.com

ISBN: 978-0-88465-397-4 (paperback)
ISBN: 978-0-88465-413-1 (ePub)
ISBN: 978-0-88465-414-8 (Mobipocket)

Library of Congress Control Number: 2015950494

Cover Design: James Bozeman
Photos copyright Mother Elisabeth (Czwikla)
http://saintelizabethskete.org
http://motherelisabeth.smugmug.com/

CONTENTS

INTRODUCTION

The acquisition of holiness does not come without persistent effort. To purify one's heart has always been a struggle, a battle with our fallen human nature. We can look back many centuries and find instructive counsels on this within the writings of the Holy Fathers; we can study the lives of saints who knew firsthand of such ascetic feats. Their experience and wisdom can encourage us to become better Christians.

Still, one may be tempted to ask: Why publish the letters of a nineteenth-century nun in the twenty-first century? What can she teach the contemporary Christian reader about spiritual discernment that has not been written elsewhere?

We live within a cultural milieu that glorifies worldly self-fulfillment. As never before, we see ourselves as architects of our own destiny, arranging most things according to our own will. Inevitably, this attitude affects our endeavors in the spiritual life as well. So often our sinful heart yearns for spiritual heights, but shuns the hardships essential for true progress within this realm. It is here that the sobriety of Abbess Arsenia's letters can dispel our fantasies of emotional self-gratification and set us on the true path toward salvation. She insists upon a consistent curbing of one's own will in order to align oneself with the will of the Lord our Saviour. It is indeed a bitter pill for us to swallow, but indispensable medicine in our self-inflated age.

Once, in a discussion during the Paschal season, Abbess Arsenia told the sisters of her community:

> We do not want to follow the word of Christ because it is harsh; it is a double-edged sword for our hearts, which are full of passions.

Labor and self-denial are essential, for only the persistent obtain the Kingdom; one needs to take it by force. No matter how deep the darkness that surrounds one's soul, one must find the way out by Christ's word, to search for Christ as the myrrh-bearers sought Him. They looked for Him, the Dead One, in the dark of night, but found the living God. And Christ is found in our hearts as well, and He is alive in the Gospel; it shines for us, showing us His image in light. Let us rouse ourselves to spiritual labor, leave laziness behind and follow the myrrh-bearers. Grant all of this to us, O Lord![1]

Abbess Arsenia's counsels are steeped in Holy Scripture and in the inspiration that she draws from the services of the Holy Orthodox Church. Many of the letters are written specifically to pass on the wisdom of her spiritual mother, Schema-nun Ardaliona, to whom Mother Arsenia entrusted her soul five years after being tonsured a riasophor nun.[2] Ever grateful for Mother Ardaliona's insight on how to truly root out the hidden passions of the heart, Abbess Arsenia writes in one of her letters:

If the acknowledgement of one's weakness and sinfulness is the beginning of faith, it is also the beginning of one's salvation. If without faith it is impossible to do God's will and follow His commandments, so it is inconceivable to acknowledge one's weakness unless one labors to fulfill God's holy laws. *Only by submitting one's will to the will of God, by resolving to walk in the way of His commandments and heading in this direction, can the soul become aware of its own weakness, its passions and the depth of its sinfulness* [emphasis added]. Instead of the love for one's neighbor that we are called to have, the soul will find in the heart only self-love; instead of the perception of God's will, it will find in the mind only self-opinion, foolishness. And how much infirmity of soul and utter lack of willpower come along with this! Only then will it begin to seek help from heaven, for through experience it will be convinced that without the help of God it is altogether powerless.[3]

   Most of the letters within this collection were written over the course of twenty years, between 1870 and 1890. In them Abbess Arsenia discusses the essentials of authentic spiritual toil with Peter Alexandrovich Brianchaninov, brother of the renowned hierarch, St Ignatius (Brianchaninov).[4] Although we read only Abbess Arsenia's side of the correspondence, we get a glimpse of the recipient of the letters and sense his thorough grasp of Orthodox asceticism. Peter eventually left his high post of governor of the region of Stavropol and joined his brother, St Ignatius, in Nikolo-Babaevskii Monastery, where he was St Ignatius's constant helper and supporter. After his brother's blessed repose in 1867, Peter was tonsured and given the name Paul. It is no wonder that Professor Alexei Osipov, a popular professor and lecturer at the Academy of the Holy Trinity-St Sergius Lavra, often suggests both the works of St Ignatius Brianchaninov and Abbess Arsenia's letters as sober guidelines for the contemporary Orthodox Christian layman.

   "Then Jesus said to His disciples, 'If anyone desires to come after Me, let him deny himself, and take up his cross, and follow Me'."[5] The way of the world and the way of the Cross can never be reconciled. May Abbess Arsenia's realistic and truthful counsels regarding salvation motivate us to forego the self-willed way of the world and press on with all diligence to follow the Gospel commandments of Christ.

Photos of Abbess Arsenia

A Short Biography

Abbess Arsenia (born Anna Mikhailovna Sebriakova) (1833–1905) was born into a prominent landowner family of the Don Region. She was only six years old when her mother died. Her father, Mikhail Vasilievich, was a well-educated, pious man. It was through his influence that Anna came to choose the monastic life. At the age of seventeen she was brought to the Ust'-Medveditskii Monastery[1] and was tonsured four years later with the name Arsenia.

Although Mother Arsenia came from a privileged background, this did not stop her from taking on the most difficult obediences at the monastery. She split wood, stoked the ovens, and washed the dishes along with the other novices. In her cell, she followed a strict prayer rule and attended all church services, despite the fact that Matins began at 3 a.m. She read the Holy Scriptures daily and learned the Psalter by heart. In studying the works of the Holy Fathers, she tried to apply their teachings to her own life.

The young monastic longed for a spiritual guide in her ascetic struggles. Her wish was granted five years after her tonsure in the person of Schema-nun Ardaliona. Behind what initially seemed like abruptness on the part of the schema-nun, Mother Arsenia found a treasure house of wisdom, for Mother Ardaliona possessed a rare gift of spiritual discernment. With her guidance, the future abbess undertook the difficult labor of cutting away the inner passions of the heart at their root.

Mother Arsenia took charge of the Ust'-Medveditskii Monastery as abbess in 1864 at the early age of thirty-one. She remained at its head for forty-one years. Under her direction the convent flourished. At times, it housed up to 860 nuns and 1,500 lay workers.[2] She organized a four-year tuition-free academic school for young women. The monastery also had an art school, a library, and even its own brick factory. During the years 1875–1885, a magnificent cathedral that could hold up to five thousand people was built in honor of the Kazan icon of Mother of God. Fifteen thousand people were present at its consecration.[3]

Before the construction of the cathedral began, Mother Arsenia met the family of Hierarch Ignatius Brianchaninov, just after his blessed repose at the Nikolo-Babaevskii Monastery in 1867. Bishop Ignatius's books on asceticism had become available in the 1860s. Mother Arsenia read them with joy. She was amazed at how his teachings corresponded to that of her own spiritual mother, Schema-nun Ardaliona. His brother, Peter, became a close friend and ardent supporter of the cathedral building project. Mother Arsenia became his spiritual mentor. It is their correspondence that makes up the bulk of this book.

Abbess Arsenia continued to live in strict asceticism. Toward the end of her life, she took on the additional toil of digging caves under her monastery, dedicating each one to a holy remembrance, such as Christ's final days before His Passion and the suffering of the Mother of God at Her Son's Crucifixion.[4] Abbess Arsenia reposed in the Lord at the Diveevo Monastery in 1905, where she had traveled to venerate the relics of St Seraphim of Sarov. The memory of this ardent laborer for Christ and His Church lives on in the hearts and minds of the Orthodox faithful of the Don Region.

PART 1

The Notes of Abbess Arsenia

Humility is the only state of the spirit through which all spiritual gifts are able to enter an individual. This is the door that opens the heart and renders it capable of receiving spiritual sensations. Humility gives the heart undisturbed rest, and brings peace and sobriety to the intellect. Humility is a power that surrounds the heart, alienating it from all worldly things and granting it a perception of eternal life, which is imperceptible to the carnal man. Humility gives the mind its original purity. It begins to see clearly the difference between good and evil, and it is able to identify each condition and movement within the heart, just as primeval Adam was able to name the beasts, each according to their particular characteristics. Humility places the seal of silence upon all that is human, and man's spirit, standing before the Lord in prayer, is receptive to His revelations . . . Before the heart achieves humility it is incapable of pure, spiritual prayer.

Our scattered thoughts engage our mind with trivial concerns, hindering a constant remembrance of God. Only when our life is wholly directed toward God do we become capable of seeing God in all and begin to do so by faith—not only in all the significant happenings of life but even in the insignificant ones—and to submit entirely to His holy will. Without this, pure, unceasing prayer is impossible. The remembrance of God—and consequently, pure prayer—are further impeded by feelings and passions. Therefore, one must strictly pay heed to the heart and all its imaginings, firmly resisting them, for such thoughts bring the soul into impenetrable darkness. Every passion causes the soul to suffer; it is a sickness and it requires immediate healing. Even despondency and other types of coldness of heart toward spiritual activity are illnesses. Just as a person recovering from a fever remains for a time weak, listless, and incapable of any work—so the soul, which is sick with a passion, becomes indifferent, weak, feeble, insensitive, and incapable of spiritual action. Such are the passions of the soul. To arm ourselves against them, to do battle with them and overcome them is our primary work. We must labor diligently in the battle against the passions of the soul. Prayer reveals to us the passions living in our soul. Whatever passion interferes with our prayer, this is the one to battle without ceasing. Prayer itself will aid in this fight, and prayer will help eradicate the passion.

The lamp with which the virgins are able to meet the Bridegroom is the Holy Spirit, who enlightens the soul, purifies it, makes it Christ-like, and renders all its attributes according to the Great Archetype. Christ recognizes such a soul as His bride, for He sees its similarity to Himself. If the soul is not enlightened by this Light, the Holy Spirit, it remains in total darkness. The enemy of God takes up his abode in this darkness, filling the soul with various passions and creating within it his own likeness. Christ does not recognize such a soul as His own and excludes it from His presence. In order for our lamp not to be extinguished we must constantly add oil, which is to say ceaseless prayer, without which the lamp cannot stay lit.

* * *

Within each soul there is a natural yearning for goodness. I think of it as a divine calling. It acts so powerfully in some souls that nothing earthly can ever satisfy them. I have always placed great value on such yearning, but today I came to realize that fear [of God] guards the soul more effectively and is just as necessary when the soul is prospering as it is when the soul is at its weakest. One comes to the fear of God by frequently remembering the hour of death and acknowledging that this may be one's last day, one's last minute on this earth. The grace of God implants this fear within the heart. "Instill Thy fear within the hearts of thy servants," prays the Holy Church.

* * *

It is impossible to achieve pure, undistracted prayer when it is not preceded by self-sacrificial action. Moreover, one must daily impress this upon one's heart and reject every deed, word, feeling, and thought that is displeasing to God. Every deed must be in line with God's commandments, every feeling subject to His word, every thought filled with His truth. By doing this, or at least striving toward this, we are able to notice any unseemly feeling or thought and to reject it by means of prayer. If our soul is thus oriented, the name of Jesus acts independently within it. It cuts off every contrary thought, suppresses every feeling unworthy of Him, enlightens the soul to the knowledge of His will, and establishes within it peace of heart and serenity of thought.

* * *

To every feeling the enemy adds his poison. Thus, to contrition over one's sins he adds despair and hopelessness, so the soul becomes despondent and weak; to renunciation—hardness of heart, coldness, and lack of feeling; to love—sensuality; to consolation through grace—vanity, etc. Man is unable to separate this poison from the positive emotions, but with the help of the Jesus Prayer, pronounced with faith and a contrite heart, this poison is isolated. With the light of Christ darkness is dispelled from the heart and the enemy's influence is exposed. By the power of Christ the enemy's activity disappears and the soul is left in its natural state—not always strong, not always purified of carnal filth, but tranquil and able to submit to the action of God's hand.

* * *

The condition of a fallen sinner wholly corresponds to the words of the Lord: "*Both thorns and thistles it [the ground] shall bring forth to you.*"[1] The ground of our heart, likewise, is constantly bringing forth passions and sins. The attempts of the soul to cleanse itself, when not enlightened by God's grace, are always difficult, laborious and ineffective. "*In the sweat of your face you shall eat bread.*"[2] With great effort and a lengthy struggle are the passions uprooted, as thorns from the ground. And again, with a little laxity, in certain situations where one gets carried away, they are ready to revive, and do so. They grow within the heart, smothering the seed of God's word, which was not even given the opportunity to take root and gather strength, let alone to bring forth fruit and nourish the soul. The spring (our intellect) has no sooner been cleansed—and that with great difficulty—than again torrents of impure thoughts pollute it, preventing the parched soul from slaking its thirst with the pure water of divine revelations. *"In the sweat of your face you shall eat bread."*[3]

The soul labors to the point of bloody sweat—as indeed it must—in order not to die of hunger. This constant and strenuous work is what prevents the regrowth of the thorns of passions; it keeps them from becoming a forest where wild animals can wander. By constant pruning and cutting, the soul regains the opportunity to feed upon the daily bread that the Great Sower plants within its soil. The Lord does not leave a man's labors without reward. He will send early and late rains, and the earth will bring forth grass, then the ears, and then wheat will fill the ears. The grace of God, when it overshadows the soul, burns up the thorns of the passions and produces fruit. *"Whosoever eats My flesh and drinks My blood has eternal life."*[4] *"Out of his heart will flow rivers of living water."*[5] . . . Only in this condition will the soul no longer thirst and have no desire to draw from earthly sources of water. Our work also consists in gradually purifying these earthly springs, in order that we might drink at least some drops of clean water, and not draw toads and other impurities from the murky waters. *"In the sweat of your face you shall eat bread,"*[6] until you are fed with that bread which comes from heaven.

* * *

"Be still, and know that I am God."[7] To accept this understanding even partially, every feeling must be erased from the heart, and every thought from the mind.

By transgressing the commandments of God, we sin before God, before others, and before our own conscience. We thus subject ourselves not only to the judgment of God, but also to human judgment. By offending God, by dishonoring Him and the image of His glory within ourselves, we are constantly hurting our neighbors, tempting them, encouraging them to sin, showing them a poor example through our sinfulness, instead of helping them to reach salvation, so we are rightfully given over to the judgment of men. This judgment—which manifests itself in the form of accusations, harsh words, slander, hatred and even leads some to feel justified in inflicting persecution, martyrdom, death upon us—we need to accept as due punishment and to always consider ourselves debtors in the eyes of our neighbors.

While we walk in the flesh, we regard our neighbor as our debtor; we demand of him not only lawful truth but grace-filled sanctity as the common property of all men. When he does not repay his debt to us, we judge him and hate him, we persecute him and torture him. However, when we are led by the Spirit, when the Spirit of God fills us with the riches of His goodness, then we seek nothing from our neighbor, we forgive him all that he owes us, and we no longer even regard him as our debtor.

Human weakness manifests itself primarily in the inconstancy to which our nature is subject. Our minds can be occupied with spiritual thoughts, and the next minute they are capable of entertaining carnal, animalistic images. Holy feelings are replaced by carnal, base ones. Peace, joy, and an ardent desire for virtue fill our soul only to give way to confusion, sadness, and despondency. This characteristic changeability is inherent in human nature. It is especially noticeable to those who, while working in God's house and before His face, are striving toward God, toward keeping their mind focused on the Jesus Prayer, their heart on the paths of His commandments, their soul at the foot of His Cross. Having come to know by experience the inconstancy of our nature, they have achieved deep humility, which prevents them from falling. They are not subject to pride during peaceful times, nor to despondency and despair in times of confusion. They have acquired the fear of God, which guards their actions, and which is ready for an onslaught even in peaceful times.

The tendency to be changeable is especially evident in one whose soul is full of fire, that is, passion. St Ignatius the God-bearer said: "I do not possess the fire of love for material things, but I have within me water which flows and cries out to me: Go to the Father." This flowing water extinguishes the flame of passion—it is the Holy Spirit.

No human virtue can extinguish this fire, or diminish its power. Virtues, when they are rightly practiced, bring forth fruit. The partaking of spiritual fruit familiarizes the soul with living sensations, pure and sweet, which deaden the desire for that which is carnal, corrupt and passionate. For example, the virtue of silence, when practiced with discernment, cuts off every useless word, thought and deed, and brings forth fruit: tranquility of mind and peace of heart. When the soul partakes of this fruit, it keeps silent, or, if it loses it, it eagerly returns to it—not because silence is a monastic rule, but because it has tasted the fruit of silence and desires its sweetness. Thus, the fruit itself, obtained through the practice of virtue, creates the incentive to live in this manner.

When perfection comes, the partial is abandoned. Once the harvest brings forth bountiful fruit, the tools of virtue are no longer needed. But for those in whom the fire of passions still burn, it is mandatory to hold fast to the path of God's commandments, to walk the path of the virtues according to His word, and, having tasted the delight of spiritual fruit, not to waste time in deviations—to which we are prone on account of our inconstancy—and not to corrupt our taste with worldly or carnal impressions. "If you have fallen, get up," as long as there is a place for the feet. "Let us press on until we reach His path."

I read St John Climacus's chapter "On Pride" and stopped at the words: "The punishment of one who is prideful is his own fall." Such punishment is wisely used by the Lord as medicine against pride. But the actions of God's Providence and his censure can only benefit a person when he strives toward eternal goals. If he has set for himself the goal of salvation—the One God—then all that happens to him will serve him well in its attainment. On being deprived of all earthly "good things," on having to bear up against personal attacks, or enduring humiliations—which would crush even a very strong soul that chooses for itself an earthly goal—the soul that loves God receives strength, wisdom, freedom. If it loses anything in these circumstances, it is the passions that had formerly ensnared it, the bindings of which it could not loosen by the will alone, which could only be destroyed by the action of God. It is a great good not to be subject to anything earthly, not even to the desires of the soul; then all the actions of God directing the soul toward salvation are effectual, killing off the passion but not the soul. In the opposite case, both the passions and the soul are destroyed. A soul that has renounced the passions becomes able to perceive virtue. Having renounced sensual pleasures, it directly experiences humility, etc. Having renounced its own desires, its sin-loving will, its own understanding, it is brought to the knowledge of God's will. Through actively fulfilling God's will, which becomes apparent through working to the benefit of one's neighbor, the soul is enlightened by divine revelations. This enlightenment leads the soul not only to purity, but to a state of dispassion.

Silence cleanses the mind of thoughts. The knowledge of one's sinfulness, one's lack of wisdom, one's powerlessness, one's inadequacy in everything brings the soul to faith. The renunciation of one's self-will leads one to active faith, which manifests itself in simplicity and humility. The first brings about purity of thought, and the second, purity of heart.

PART 2

The Letters to Peter Alexandrovich Brianchaninov

LETTER NO. 1   *October 7, 1870*

I generally do not like to confine myself to secular correspondence, but like to share my thoughts and feelings with those who are able to understand and empathize with them, even in writing. Your letter brought me comfort. You remember me, and that is endearing. However, for God's sake I ask you, do not exalt me so; it is unfair, and I excuse your words by the fact that your spiritually orphaned emotion wanted to see me in this way . . . you imagined that you are seeing the familiar characteristics of a dear, lofty, holy image which sanctified your soul through your encounter with it. Let us contemplate such an image in God's great and wondrous creation, but for myself I would desire some knowledge of my own weaknesses and sinfulness, and ask that you entreat the Lord, the Giver of good things, to grant this on my behalf.

LETTER NO. 2   *November 2, 1870*

I thoroughly believe that God's will is revealed to us through the circumstances that surround us. I see that the current situation dictates an escape to the mountains, but as I regard today's circumstance, I see that this indication is incomplete . . . I long for a life totally removed from all things earthly, and therefore my soul longs for it rather insistently at times. I am afraid to be affected by this strong emotion, for this may not be the right time, and may be profitable only at some appointed time in the future . . .

9

The other day I received the fifth volume[1] from A. V. How good of you to add the portrait of Bishop Ignatius to this volume! The Lord enlightened you to do so, and the portrait is such a good one! At present I am reading this volume as I would the sayings of the Holy Fathers, and even one look at Vladyka's holy face is a great comfort to me. While contemplating this image, one is more able to concentrate. Thoughts come together and an ability to confess all the subtle disorders of one's heart appears when those prophetic eyes look into the depths of the soul.

LETTER NO. 3   *November 7, 1870*

The path to salvation is cruel, as are the words that are sometimes spoken of it. They are as a two-edged sword that cuts out our passions, our emotionality, and sears our heart with pain as they are being carved out. Will the time ever come when there is nothing left for that sword to do? No, there will always be a job left for it, there is no end to our spiritual cleansing, and in every heart there will be found a particle of dirt that needs to be removed. In myself I see it as a sign of lack of fervency when my heart ceases to ache and fight—it is a symptom of intense darkening. When this darkness is chased away by the word of God, the heart aches, for no enlightenment is possible without pain—for in that case, it is surely fantasy.

LETTER NO. 4   *February 6, 1871*

I rejoice and thank the Lord that He vouchsafed me, a sinner, to pass on the teaching of my mother, Schema-nun Ardaliona, the teaching which gives life to my soul. Pafnutia and I are taken aback, seeing the extent to which you find empathy with the words of our mother, and with our spirit. The power of truth is a living power that communicates itself to souls, joining them into one image. May the Lord give strength to us all, and may He help us to exist in the Truth, which is He Himself, and the path to Him is through our weakness, through the fullness of our sinfulness. Yes, this is not the path of lies, not one that was invented, for the Lord Himself said not to seek Him in any particular state (of mind, body, or soul[2]), but that He will appear to us. And so He appears, bringing peace, strength, and light into a soul that is perishing, weak, and dark. When we chase after certain conditions, then we are attempting to catch a fantasy. I thoroughly feel my weakness, and sometimes become despondent, but know from experience that when this weakness reaches its limits, so that no hope is left for any activity, or any rational solution, then, in that very moment and only at that moment, one spiritually apprehends a special help from God, or, better said, the knowledge of Him and the power of His action in the soul. I do not ask for strength from anyone, being afraid to awaken my own self-reliance, that poison which is spilled onto every human good work, and for this reason, I am overwhelmed by my own vibrant weakness. Yet it is this weakness that can elicit that living Power, which is the only one that my soul yearns after. In such a state, a great fear grips the soul, for perdition is in it and all that surrounds it, but salvation is in that Will, which the soul finds the audacity to perceptibly comprehend and influence by its pleas. Fear fills it to the uttermost depths.

LETTER No. 5 *February 13, 1871*

The Lord sends us sorrows in this world, and these sorrows snatch us away from earth, or better said, from the attachment to all which is earthly. For this reason even sorrows are a gift from God. Why do we not accept them with the same gratitude as we accept joys? Does this not stem from the sinfulness of our heart, our inability to deny ourselves and seek only God's will?

You may have noticed that I avoid speaking about prayer, because I myself have not mastered it. Yet I do not want to leave your questions unanswered and will lay out my understanding in the hope that you will correct it if you see a fault. I said "Thou Thyself art the salvation of my soul"—I said it, and literally state this, believing that this is so, but to fully understand this is higher than our capability. You say, "The assimilation of the name of Jesus by the soul is already its salvation." No, something is not right here. The salvation of the soul is in God's strength, which acts upon our soul through this Name, when it fully comprehends the state of its sinfulness. Vladyka said it well when he advised us not to accept thoughts during prayer and, above all, not to trust them. When the heart begins to sympathize with the mind, moving from a state of self-consciousness to a feeling of spiritual contriteness, then various comprehensions enter the soul, and they do not exist in the mind, and therefore cannot be termed thoughts, but comprehensions, or visions; they can be genuine and outside of time, but become the property of the soul, taking it out of its usual state and bringing it to higher understanding. Yet all of this is of God, but as for us, all that is natural for us is to acknowledge our sinfulness and to have faith in the Lord Who saves us, upon Whom we need to call in humility, leaving even our salvation itself to His will. During the prayer rule I try to confine my mind to the Jesus Prayer. Sometimes, when I am very distracted and inattentive, I turn my mind to the reading of canons to the Mother of God and the saints, but it is in the intent to turn my attention to prayer, not to turn my attention from prayer to reading. When the mind has turned to prayer, it is possible to attentively follow reading, not forsaking prayer. If our prayer had less emotionality, everything would accelerate it, yet as it is sometimes canons and church services get in the way, and we need dark cells to gather our thoughts, such as mine which is in the garden, which I call my "weakness," and complete silence. Yet these are temporary tools; nothing helps me as much as life itself. Even though the goal is the renunciation of life, the path toward which is self-sacrificial fulfillment of God's commandments, the law of sinfulness points each action toward its own goal, and the soul is greatly grieved in this battle. The Lord, healing the weakness of emotionality with the bitter circumstances of life, by the measure of renouncement gives the soul invisible strength and the knowledge of His Providence. It is there that I learn of my own weakness and the knowledge of the Lord; it is there that the Lord frees me of heaviness and communicates spiritual comprehensions, so life itself teaches me even to pray. I believe that a pure heart is necessary for prayer, and it is acquired by living a life of self-sacrifice according to God's commandments.

Letter No. 6   *February 20, 1871*

The pain in my left hip escalated to its upper limit. I suffered greatly for three days. Yesterday, however, I was much better and I decided to copy out some lenten stichera, which I like to sing to myself in hours of despondency. . . . The Lenten Triodion was brought and I, not getting out of bed, copied several of my favorites. Only when I was finished did I notice that they begin with the weeping of Adam and end with the weeping of the harlot—yet what a difference between the two! These are two very different states of man's soul, even though the last proceeds from the first and is its fruit, its perfection, but between the two there is an entire journey of labor, battle, asceticism, not always intense, not one that always wins. In the first, one hears the realization of sin—the first step toward repentance and therefore such fear is heard in that repentful cry, coupled with a light despair. In the second, there is apparent hatred of sin, love, and audacity. This latter condition is possible only when the soul not only hears, but sees the Lord Jesus saving it and draws near to Him, Who has come to save it, one which is deadened by sin.

In answer to your letters I wish to say much, but my strength fails me today and I am afraid I will not finish what I started. I will say one thing, however: you often, as you remember death, state your soul's longing—that during those frightening moments you may receive aid from people whom you admire. This desire is so strong that it searches for reassurance that this will surely happen. By God's mercy so it will be, if during life your soul is not deprived of contact with those souls whose help is required. Yet for myself and for you I do not wish such an insistent desire, this firm conviction. I am afraid to tell the All-knowing Lord that He give me such-and-such this hour, then something else at an appointed time. I am afraid to delve into His saving Will and choose that which is profitable for me. And though I constantly call upon the prayers of my eldress, and the prayers of all the unified souls of fathers and mothers who are on their way to salvation to help my sinful soul and thus am strengthened and supported, I am nonetheless wary of finding conviction in anything, and even love this state of helplessness, for it creates fear in the soul, which shakes it to its depths and it vividly feels itself in God's power, Whose will it does not dare to fathom.

May the Lord help you pass the time of lent, the time of solitude with benefit for the soul, so that its weakness and sinfulness would become more apparent and the Help that comes be felt more acutely.

LETTER NO. 7   *March 10, 1871*

The reason I wished to destroy my notes is because they are mine, and I trust little of what I write myself. One can speak of one's limited experience in life, but it is dangerous to write about it, for together with the truth some falsehood may be added which is still alive in the soul, and will cause harm instead of benefit. I am returning the sheet to you. Having so many words of spiritual experience of grace-filled and holy persons, is it necessary to add to them that which sometimes is revealed to the blind eye of an unclean soul? Being conscious of this fully and fearing that falsehood may be mixed in with the truth, which was passed on to me by my matushka, I ask you to check my words against the sayings of the fathers, and if you see incorrectness, be kind enough to point it out to me. Once you asked, is it possible to pass my words and understanding on to the father archimandrite? For at times this is appropriate to do as you speak of matters relating to yourself. It seems to me that I remember during our conversations I mentioned that when it comes to our spiritual discussions and about spiritual counsel in general, what you have heard, read, or experienced, it is best to be relayed only when a real need arises; if it is passed on just as a novel idea which has astounded your mind, I consider this unnecessary and even harmful. However, with regard to father archimandrite, the situation is different. You may share all you want with him, whatever it is useful for you to say, but I do request one thing: pass on his reactions to my words back to me. I hold his spiritual opinions in high esteem and will even say to you that if you share my thoughts with him, I will share them more freely and in more detail with you, for my fear that they may confuse you, or if an error be found in them has lessened, since it will be made apparent (by the father archimandrite's reaction).[3] I only ask you to pass on everything that you think or hear about my words, for I would rather that they not be passed on without my knowledge. If time allows and I am in the mental state for writing, then my next letter will arrive shortly, and it will be written without any reservations.

LETTER NO. 8   *March 20, 1871*

The day of February 8th, as I recall and as you described it, gave you direct knowledge of the helpless and weak state of the soul that lives in the hope of salvation through the One God. If you remember my words then, you probably understand that constantly acquiring such a state is the goal itself. Of course, it can occur in various degrees and appear in many forms, but the spirit of our entire life is full faith in God coupled with complete distrust of oneself. For this reason I do not totally empathize with your constant complaint that you do not have the desired virtues, that you notice and even feel the battle inside yourself from your weak state. As I see it, not only should you humble yourself in your mind at that moment, but for days and weeks one should confine oneself in that situation, to feel the confinement of one's soul, which lacks the strength to change this state of perdition. Only then is living faith in the Lord Who saves us possible.

Somewhere else you wrote that you see sinfulness within yourself, and imagine within yourself passions and sins as innumerable serpents. No, this is not seen through the imagination, never through it, but is revealed in the heart by degree of selflessness. Your quotes and words of Vladyka, which you passed on concerning the Name of Jesus Christ, were wholly correct and brought contrition to my soul. But to fully grasp this Name, along with the Lord Himself Incarnate, is the highest of revelations, and is given to the soul in its own time, a soul that has thoroughly experienced the path of the Gospel commandments, which has reached a measure of perfection. I do not dare to speak of God's revelations, but even in our labor there must be order and consequence, to regard oneself realistically, at the same time through faith not to strive for the heights above which there is an impenetrable curtain.

To you the difference between the weeping of Adam and that of the harlot seemed a novelty. That surprises me. You know, of course, of the path of repentance, and consequently, there are different degrees, paths, and ways to perfection on this journey. One must take care not to self-assuredly skip over certain steps, and standing on the bottom rung one must not seek that which is found on the top. This is why I said that between these two states is an entire life of *podvig* (spiritual struggle) and battle. Nothing is more useful to man than to know one's own situation, where he is on this path. Then he will make no mistakes and will be heading in the right direction. In this it is essential to have a guide, who will truthfully reveal the state and situation of his pupil. I remember, when

I began to live with matushka, and listened to her advice on the path of salvation, I, as if seeing this path from beginning to end, would often ask her: "where am I?" and matushka would answer that I am nowhere, because there is nothing in me which would indicate a commitment to salvation, not even a living acknowledgment of perdition, which then, in turn, would prod me on to seek salvation. I admit that at the time I did not fully understand matushka's words, although I believed her and bemoaned my state. Afterward I acutely felt their truthfulness and now they serve me, as all her words, as a basis for self-reflection.

LETTER No. 9   *March 22, 1871*

Your letter of March 8–11 reminded me that I have not answered a question for which you have been awaiting an answer for a long time. When I said, "the path to the Lord is through our sinfulness" I did not mean the "Kingdom of God which is within" a person. This eternal promise of God is fulfilled in unblemished holy hearts and is the end of things sought. As I said those words I thought just as people's sins, the insufficiency of all mankind was the reason for the unfathomable and merciful descent of the Lord to our earth in order to save mankind, so in every soul the same coming of the Lord needs to be preceded by complete humility and denial of self; and for the cultivation of faith in the Saviour—the full acknowledgment of one's sinfulness and weakness, a full awareness of such an inner state, contrition, and fear. This is why I said that the path to Him is in us, and what is there within us besides sinfulness? If it is fully realized, if one truthfully understands one's soul, one finds no support aside from faith, and one will see salvation in nothing but the One Who Saves. I said, "the path is within us" because often the soul takes a sideways path and seeks it not within, but in something related to itself. Through truthful self-assessment, one inevitably comes to the Lord, but seeking Him in one's good works, labors, and such will not find Him, the Only One Who Saves, but will find oneself instead. This not only happens in general, but is manifested in occasional diversions toward doing things for the sake of self.

Yesterday I thought of looking in "The Ladder" and I read the Word to Pastors. While reading the end of this epistle I was thinking of you.

The gradations of seeing God are explained, according to the measure of the purity of one's soul: (1) chapter 15 p. 360, through the rejection of carnal life and self-love the knowledge of truth is revealed; (2) p. 361–362, upon reaching control over all passions comes the enlightenment of one's spiritual knowledge; (3) p. 363, the peace of the heart and vision of Christ the God of peace comes from active following of Him and the keeping of His commandments. Yet these are only words which cannot express that which is higher than words, higher than natural understanding and human experience, as Vladyka noted in his treatise "The Dew" (Vol. 1, p. 367). To seek any of these states within oneself is sheer folly. What can a soul tainted with sin expect besides mercy? Yet all the gifts of God, salvation and mercy for the soul we receive through Jesus Christ, the One Mediator between God and man, and so we entreat Him with faith, without fathoming Who He is, without contemplation. The rejection of self-love and faith lead the soul into simplicity and instill in it an unwavering conviction of one's nothingness, which does not alter whether God manifests His mercy, in revelation to the soul in the realm of thought, in concentration and contrition in prayer, or when one feels total coldness, lack of concentration, and even distraction. It is strange that both in the first and second case that conviction remains unchanged, although the state of the soul changes, and from this unwavering state there comes a stability of spirit that does not exalt itself in a good state nor does it plummet in a poor one. For in both these situations, the person is one and the same: a sinner in need of the mercy of the Lord. Too much attention to one's condition may bring activity to the level of emotions, not spirit, for it is the emotions that fluctuate, such is their character. This means that one must not pay much attention to thoughts, or feelings. One thing must be known—they are sinful, unclean, and cannot be otherwise, because they come from a polluted mind and heart, and it is impossible to expect anything better; for our purity and salvation, purification, and sanctification is the One Lord. From this dual faith—in one's sinfulness and God's constancy—comes a stability of spirit in the believer.

I say nothing of prayer, because I think that my words regarding the spirit serve as an answer to the question regarding prayer. When the spirit is directed in a proper way, prayer becomes its very breath, essential and effectual. As for the quietness of thought and feelings of peace—these are given to a soul that clings to Him in faith and prayer: to take this by force or establish it on one's own is impossible, and one should not strive much in this direction. Father archimandrite was correct in saying that one should not delve deeply into theological question; this is not salvific, but even harmful, and fine analysis can bring one to error, or a correct interpretation to pride. If my own opinion here is needed, to test its correctness, then I would say that the desire for salvation is the single activity of the human spirit that is essential for salvation. It is not what saves a person, but it is an essential condition in order to be saved. It comes through God's beckoning and it is strengthened by the power of God, yet even so, it comes from the human being himself, weak as he is, as all that is human. Enough has been said for the moment.

LETTER NO. 10   *April 14, 1871*

Now I would like to pass on to you one concept which I beg you not to reject despite my inability to phrase it well. This concept will serve as an answer to some of your questions. The Holy Fathers in their spiritual entreaties often urge us to seek wisdom from the Lord if we are lacking it, strength when we grow weak, patience when we are overcome with grief, and to ask the Lord for everything to our benefit. Yet I, in our conversation, said that it is best to ask for nothing but mercy, which you seemed to disagree with. Now I wish to tell you that though I do not reject that which the fathers suggest, I fear to apply their every suggestion to myself personally. The activity that I wish to speak about brings one to the acceptance of everything from the Lord, even more than this—to the acceptance by the soul of the Lord Himself, in Whom it finds everything. You already know from experience what power the soul finds in the confession that in the Lord and in Him alone is salvation, that He Himself is salvation. This confession can be professed by a soul that is fully aware of its sinfulness. You feel vibrant strength in these words, and it cannot be otherwise. During prayer this confession seems to establish the attitude of the soul, mortified by sin toward the Lord Who saves. If a soul remains constantly and deeply in this state, it begins to pray even without words, even in sleep. This confession involves the entire soul and an entire lifetime. Since the soul consists of various parts, life unfolds in various states (I speak here of spiritual life), and so this confession, preserving its single basic character, is also separated into stages.

For example, when there is no spiritual insight, when the mind is clouded, and there is no penetration into the word of God, nor into one's state, the soul confesses; "Thou, O Lord—art the One Wisdom and Enlightenment for us." When the spirit is weak: "Thou, O Lord, art my strength!" When inner darkness fills the entire person, and, as you say, one cannot penetrate inside oneself: "Thou, O Lord, art the One Light." In all other cases, similar confessions are in order. From these individual confessions comes one full and living knowledge—the knowledge of the one Redeemer, who is the only salvation for the soul. However, these private confessions should not be used superfluously, nor should one change needlessly into another; rather, they should be the expression of a great need of the soul, so that the soul finds in the Lord and in Him alone that which it lacks within itself, which it dares not even to seek within itself. These confessions are not requests for anything, no; the soul does not even want for itself nor does it want to see within itself something virtuous— it wants to see it in the One God alone, and is enlightened through faith. I will repeat again, that the soul, in every state, once it is placed in the correct relationship toward the saving Lord, through prayerful calling out of His Name, is able to perceive His vibrant power. However, these confessions cannot simply be thought about in the mind, or construed through the imagination, or immersed in feelings; they must be elicited by the need of the soul without any sudden action or heated emotion. When the morbidity of the soul is felt, I do not try to enliven it with anything: "Lord! Thou art the life of my soul, only in Thee is life eternal!" and I thus call upon His All Holy Name, and arise from my mortal state, not seeking life within myself, not desiring it for myself; is it not enough for my soul just to believe and confess as I do, that the Lord is alive, and so then, my soul will live! And it is somehow comfortable to persist in this mortal state, in order to see life in Him alone. This is not a feeling, or imagery, but a condition one stays in for days, months, years.

LETTER No. 11   *May 22, 1871*

... I will answer all your questions as briefly as possible, in order to allow myself the liberty to answer in more detail later that which I find especially important and necessary.

You do not fully understand the inner activity I described, which you called my favorite, having read it in an excerpt from the works of Gregory the Sinaite, and you wish to receive an explanation of the words you do not understand. In time the Lord will grant you to understand, and to me, through Matushka's prayers, to express her word more clearly. Now, however, the most important thing is for you to relate correctly to the word you have heard. If the word that I have passed on seems true to you, then that is enough—belief in a truth that is accepted, even if not fully comprehended, imparts that accepted truth to the soul. The Divine Teacher told His disciples: *"You are already clean because of the word which I have spoken to you."*[4] Every truthful concept based on His Divine Word participates in this same power. Truth, accepted with faith, cleanses one from the errors the soul was in, by which the soul lived. To enter any kind of spiritual activity by force is very dangerous. To attain an understanding of any spiritual matter by force is impossible. In order to understand fully (or even partially) someone's spirit, one must see and converse with him; it is impossible to gauge this correctly through the words of another. As far as you are concerned, there is nothing to be upset about with me. If your spirit is troubled, it is better to refrain from proximity without analyzing one's spiritual state. I upset you by praising you; forgive me! Yet is there cause to be upset? I do not believe that this is a condition of the soul that one needs to guard against. If there is something positive, it is impossible not to see it, one cannot but recognize it as something good; but one can and must ascribe it to the Lord, and thereby reveal a new reason for the soul to humble itself and stand in awe before the One Who is Holy and Saves. Praise, when accepted on a simple human level and as self-affection, can be beneficial, as encouragement for the despondent spirit. It used to happen with Matushka that I would feel despondency of spirit from an understanding and feeling of my complete sinfulness and weakness, and I would go to Matushka with the request that she praise me and assure me of my ability to attain salvation. Matushka would in fact begin to affirm this, so seriously and forcefully that I believed her and was comforted, and gained confidence. She was not afraid of indulging the self, but would use this as a tool to save one from the despondency that is sometimes brought about by the power of the enemy. Thus, through the action of both left and right, is our salvation achieved.

LETTER NO. 12

[Letter No. 12 was too short to be included here.]

LETTER NO. 13   *June 7, 1871*

I long to respond to your questions, the purpose of which was to expand
or explain what I wrote about in my letter of April 13. However, I have
somehow become distracted and busy and have not chosen enough free
time to write you a letter of spiritual content. This upsets me, knowing
that you are expecting an answer from me. I even had a dream last night in
which you came to visit me and I complained to you of my distracted life,
asking you to take note and remember that we should discuss my letter of
April 13 another time, when I have more time. This demonstrates that I
am concerned about answering you, even though I have not done so.

(1) You ask me to give some explanation of how to enter the activity of
     which I speak. But entering it is impossible. That activity is given to
     someone so that he would lose everything, so that he would nowhere
     and in nothing find hope for salvation. If this first condition is fully
     met, then there is hardly any need to answer the remaining questions.

(2) You ask: With what should the mind or attention be occupied, when
     thoughts are given the freedom to draw us into the abyss, and so on?
     They draw us there because we lack the strength and ability to hold
     on to them. It is as if the mind, attention, and all its powers do not
     really exist. It is not in the mind, in the memory, or in the attention,
     but rather deep in the soul that the perception that there is a Saviour
     begins. I call this perception faith because it is not the product of the
     mind, but the living sensation of the soul—therefore it is called liv-
     ing faith, even if it is very small and weak.

(3) How is faith expressed? It is expressed in not allowing one to seek
     life and the salvation of one's soul in anything. It does not allow even
     the soul to act on its own and for itself. The Jesus Prayer is an expres-
     sion of the living perception of faith.

(4) How is one's perception of the commandments and faith in the Law
     of God expressed? The soul, having nothing outside itself and in itself
     that it can hope on, and having recognized both the falseness and

lawlessness of all its own laws (worldly and human) and the insufficiency of its own powers to adhere to them, finds in God's will alone the pure and holy law that pulls the human essence out of the mire. This recognition is given to the soul that renounces all the conjectures of its own mind about it. This law is given to the soul in the providential will of God, in the word of God, and in its fullness and perfection in Jesus.

(5) You say: "If this is expressed by the confession of the One Saviour, then I am not surprised if this confession leads to prayer." Oral confession leads to oral prayer, not to say sensual. But the confession within a soul that has renounced everything, a life's confession, indeed leads to prayer. Do not be scandalized if I say that, on the path of this activity, it is not always possible to remain faithful to the activity of attentive prayer, but everything gets lost; one gets lost sometimes during the labor of prayerful activity. Jesus is the beginning and end, the goal, the limit of all human longings. He is the door by which one enters the spiritual life; He is the path leading to life. He is life itself; one who has tasted of Him will be dead to everything else. Until this very last minute, man is unable to die to everything, but by faith he can and must lose everything before coming to the Door that opens onto the path that so few are able to find.

More on the Law: The other day the Epistle of the Apostle Paul to the Romans concerning the Law was read during the Liturgy. This reading continued for several days. The more the Law required, the weaker man became. Through it sinfulness was revealed and, finally, the total inability to fulfill it. The Lord Jesus Christ put sin to death in Himself and did away with the righteousness of the Law, which destroyed man, and communicated to him the law of grace, life, and freedom, which was revealed through Him. I cannot articulate it, but that is what I felt as I listened to the Apostolic Epistle. The law that gives life, not death, was opened to me. Besides, what can the memory bear apart from the name of Jesus?

LETTERS NO. 14 AND 15

[Letters No. 14 and 15 are related to specific events of the time that were deemed not relevant for the reader today.]

LETTER No. 16   *September 10, 1871*

On September 8, all my people gathered at my place and drank tea in the room near the guest room—it is very small—and I sat and lay on the bed. Some were on chairs, others on benches, others on crates, some simply on the floor—everyone was comfortable. We talked. The general consensus demanded that I indicate what is needed for salvation, and what the salvation of the soul is. This request elicited my favorite topic, encouraging me to pass on to them that which alone is necessary, the one thing needful, that which alone can grant salvation and life to the spirit, the single goal of all souls and all angelic spirits—that is, the Lord. In order that all might attain that single goal, however, it is necessary that everything in the soul be united by the One Who is sought; an all-encompassing labor is needed so that the soul works on all things, is involved in all things, and yet denies itself in everything. It needs to seek the Lord in everything, to seek the goodness that leads to Him, and to deny itself and turn away from that evil that causes it to grow cold toward the Lord and return to a state of selfishness. At this point, it was impossible for me not to speak of those snares that the enemy sets up for human souls, leading them astray and away from salvation. He, the former Lucifer, knows what glory and blessedness man is called to, and uses all his strength to interfere with the fulfillment of the will of God in the salvation of man. He mixes his own sweetness into evil in order to ensnare our souls, and we love this sweetness of the enemy, and it replaces eternal blessedness. It is best for us to grow to love, I said, the bitterness of spiritual struggle, the malady of rejection, and through such bitterness and malady evade the captivity of the enemy, thereby reaching the path that leads to the one goal, to the one salvation, to which righteous souls and spirits seek in all eternity.

It is unfortunate that your relationship with A. Z. has become so tense. There is something in her that might serve as a great asset in your friendship toward her—this is her seeking of the Lord. As for me, whatever her situation might be, I am only human; there is nothing to be sought from me, and contact with me is as inconstant and false as I am myself. What is foremost is contact with the Lord, and in Him alone is the communion of souls eternal. For this reason it is best not to avoid her;

you need only trust her desire for salvation and help her in this quest: at times you can strengthen her desponding spirit with the strength of faith; at other times, you can awaken in her the striving for salvation, explaining the benefit of renouncing that which makes up earthly existence and its comforts, and so on. In terms of A. Z., you must likewise cultivate love for one's neighbor, that love that does not seek one's own benefit, but the benefit and salvation of one's neighbor.

LETTER No. 17   *September 21, 1871*

Do not hesitate to write to me both often and at length; this will never burden me. And even if it does, why should you concern yourself with that? Are we not called to labor? Is not labor our true occupation? May the Lord preserve us from matters that are entertaining, comforting, pleasant, and sweet (as I put it). I would not want to deprive myself of labor.

LETTER No. 18   *October 5, 1871*

I am not responding to all your spiritual questions, since I hope to see and speak with you soon. Today I will say only one thing: that confessing the Lord as the One Who Saves, as a spiritual activity, can be taken on by the soul not only over the course of hours or days, but even of years. I do not say that it replaces prayer, but the soul can abide in this state for a long time without moving on to prayer, if prayer does not come of itself. When there is no prayer due to laziness and distraction, one needs to seek it with effort; when prayer leaves us due to the rise of passions within us, we need to struggle and renounce the source of passions; when due to despondency and inner darkness the soul does not find prayer, it is best to abide in the confession of the only One Who Saves.

LETTER No. 19   *November 30, 1871*

Our flock is slowly increasing: yesterday another novice was accepted under our direction, after a year-long testing of her strivings and ours. In the convent the conviction has solidified that it is so difficult to come under my spiritual direction that it is best not even to try; she who does try, however, does so with her whole soul. Why have I so limited access to myself? Because the path is very narrow. Narrow in the sense that it demands total renunciation; narrow in the sense that it does not allow one to see any support on this path either within oneself or from those who are nearby; even more narrow in that in me, the supposed mentor, one frequently sees a branch swaying in the wind, one that often bends down to the very earth and is nearly broken. In a mentor one likes to see a firm staff upon which one can lean at any time. This I cannot provide, nor do I want to provide it. It is sufficient for the mentor to point out where to seek that staff, and blessed is the soul who finds it: the unwavering staff of support in the One Mighty and Unchangeable, Ever-living Lord.

LETTER No. 20   *December 10, 1871*

I am awaiting a letter from you informing me that solitude, prayer, reading, and the entire monastery environment have brought you spiritual calm and strengthened your forces to take up anew the work of salvation, and that in this work you felt a resurgence of faith, that has taken the place of selfishness, broken by weaknesses. Yes, humility bears good fruit. In the recognition of its sinfulness, the soul in faith perceives the Lord. But in the state of selfishness, what can the soul see and know beside itself? What can the "me" in us give, no matter how good and adorned with good works it is? Neither light, nor life. In it is a dreadful power that battles against all the commandments of God, against one's neighbors, against God Himself; a power that kills the very soul, depriving it of goodness, life, God. In moments of rest, it is difficult to discern what kind of spirit directs all the actions of man, even the benevolent ones, even in his yearning for salvation, for good-ness, for God. But it is during the time of temptation that one discov-ers that which had been unclear. If the Lord directs the soul, then the period of temptations will be a time of victory and crowns for the soul, a time of great flourishing. However, if selfishness directs one's actions, then during the time of temptation its power is unleashed against the soul itself, tormenting it as a captive and taking it to the very depths of hell. Nonetheless, these moments are better than imaginary calm. At such times the soul can correctly understand its own condition, not being fooled by its imagined goodness, and it will not consider its mental images to be its own possession. In such blessed times, if only it properly reacts to everything, the soul can sink very, very low. If it agrees to love its lowliness, its total poverty, if it gives preference to its neighbor and the Lord—finding joy in the fact that He alone is lofty and that others of its own kin have drawn nigh unto Him—then it will experience comfort from a goodness that is not borne of selfishness, but of its destruction. When I say to you that it is necessary to feel extreme poverty sometimes, I say this in general. I do not know your present condition and I acknowledge that I do not even understand how such a state of complete poverty could have come about. I am thinking, have I offended you in some way? Father Archimandrite is right when he says that I am too strict with you. He does anything but praise me for this. I would go even further: with respect to you, I take upon myself that which is not mine to take. Please forgive me this boldness, and as a gesture of forgiveness tell me what you hold against me. Only total candor can eliminate the awkwardness I notice in you. Pray for me, the greatly sinful one, yet one who wishes you all things beneficial and salvific.

LETTER No. 21   *January 1, 1872*

I congratulate you with the New Year, wishing you health, peace of soul, and renewal of life. Arsenius the Great would say each day: "Lord, I have done nothing good; grant that at least today I can make a beginning!" As for us, let us at least every New Year start anew, with renewed striving of soul to renounce all that is old in us, that we may enter into communion with that new and renewed nature to which resurrection is promised. Grant, O Lord, that we may begin anew, and begin anew more and more often!

LETTER No. 22   *March 4, 1872*

Now you are already in Petersburg. May the Lord bless you and help you to labor for the good of truth! You fear distraction in meeting your relatives and acquaintances. Such distraction will of course come, but it need not frighten you. While we sit in our cells we battle with passionate and sinful thoughts; but when among people we battle with the passions themselves. So it is essentially the same, although in the latter case the battle is more extensive, vivid, and real. In our cells we study the Word of God; among people we should strive to fulfill it. In the sitting rooms of Petersburg the commandments of God can be fulfilled in deed, so do not fret that you were unable to copy them out of the Gospel. They will be fulfilled when you place your soul on the path of self-sacrifice, when the purpose of your activity is self-denial. This condition of soul will in itself dictate what should transpire in your relationships with people and with those close to you. Right away it will find the middle way that is foreign to the saccharine and the need to please, yet is equally foreign to coldness, cruelty, and hardness. That middle way is love. It is no misfortune if you get carried away at times and grow weak; but it is a misfortune if you leave the place in which I have advised you to stand. Blessed self-sacrifice! Abiding in it, one will not be burned amidst flames or be drowned in water, whereas with selfishness one can perish not only in one's solitary cell, but even in Paradise itself.

LETTER NO. 23   *March 8, 1872*

During the first week [of lent] we prepared for Holy Communion, and on Sunday I had the urge to speak with my daughters. A group of about ten gathered and we discussed, among other things, love for one's neighbor. We need to put our neighbor where we ourselves are standing; which means that first we must step aside from the place where we are standing. Where is that place we are standing? It is the whole world, visible and invisible. Everywhere, selfishness has taken everything for itself, and wants to leave nothing for its neighbor. How can the soul love its neighbor when it feels that he is taking everything away from it, having the same rights to everything as it? Therefore the soul perceives him as his enemy and hates him. We must take everything away from ourselves in order to give everything to our neighbor. Then, along with the neighbor, the soul will find the Lord.

LETTER No. 24   *April 5, 1872*

Today I read one homily in the book by Isaac the Syrian and was so satisfied and consoled by it that I closed the book. He says: "for one who is
faithful, love for God is sufficient consolation even in his ruin." I hope
these words will console you as well, giving you strength even in your
very weakness.

LETTER No. 25   *April 15, 1872*

On the eve of the bright feast of Pascha, I write you and congratulate you
and wish you to meet it with spiritual joy. We have not prepared ourselves as we ought, even in the smallest possible way, in order to rejoice in
spirit; but the very event that is commemorated in the upcoming feast is
so great and beneficial that it acts joyfully and brightly even in darkness.

LETTER No. 26   *January 23, 1873*

I thank you and all those who are close to me in spirit, all those who
have suffered along with me. Common love and common prayer have
touched God's mercy: my illness, it seems, has subsided. Of course, I am
far from saying that my illness has passed, and I think it will still require
prolonged treatment and care; but it has diminished to such an extent
that there are hours when I forget that the sickness lives in me, and
I live and act as healthy people live and act. Father Archimandrite left
us on the 22nd. His visit gave me much, very much, comfort. The more
I get to know him, the more I see the fruits of proper spiritual guidance
in him. My soul rests in conversation with him, and his capacity for self-
sacrifice amazes me and strengthens my feeble spirit. Alongside all that
is good in him, there is in him such a potential for spiritual ascent that
I do not know the measure of his future spiritual accomplishment, if the
Lord finds it pleasing to prolong his bodily and spiritual life. I say all
this to you alone—he does not like it when I prophesy something to him
beyond the awareness of my own sinfulness, but it is this very awareness
that is the foundation from which a soul should never depart. For if it
loses it, not only will it gain nothing more, but it will lose the path leading to good.

LETTER NO. 27   *February 16, 1873*

You will receive this letter during Great Lent and this will be very appropriate, because at this time you will likely be more inclined to forgive your neighbor. I ask your forgiveness by means of this letter, inasmuch as I am writing it at the end of Cheesefare week, in the days assigned by the Orthodox Church for asking forgiveness. There is always cause for asking forgiveness of one other, and I find solace when I consider myself guilty. I am guilty before you in that I frequently demand of you that which I myself lack—forgive me.

LETTER NO. 28   *February 20, 1873*

I congratulate you with the approaching forty-day fast, which I hope you will pass in perfect health and spiritual struggle. We, according to the monastery custom, say "with benefit for the soul," yet the benefit is not from us, but from the Lord—and for this we will entreat the Lord's mercy. I wish for you to remain in spiritual struggle, because struggle is from us; we need to abide in it constantly, and now the time facilitates it and the Church helps. In what should this struggle consist? What is its purpose? Struggle should consist of awakening the body from sleepiness, from laziness, so that it would stand vigilantly during church services and during the prayer rule in one's cell; in sobering up the soul from despondency, the mind from idle thoughts, and the heart from passionate feelings, so that the whole inner man can stand before the Lord. This is the goal of all struggles. Will the Lord allow us to reach this desired goal? This, again, is not for us to discuss, but leaving this struggle would be sinful. Only despondency, fortified by unbelief and based on amusement, can make one neglect it, making its goal the fulfillment of one's passionate desires. It is not good that you fall into great despondency through the onslaught of temptations. Cast aside your confusion; I do not want to see this in you! Thoughts of hopelessness are from the enemy, and I do not want you to listen to his suggestions. The Lord will not allow us to perish. He will conquer the enemy and our passions. He will grant us eternal salvation through His unconquerable mercy. I believe in this and, knowing your soul, do not see any reason why you, too, should not have this faith, full and unchanging. Our weaknesses will not destroy us, but our unbelief can destroy us, from which may the Lord protect us through His mercy.

LETTER NO. 29   *March 2, 1873*

You have been reading Peter of Damascus. Yes, I remember that I wanted to read his work together with you, not so much in order to read Damascene himself, but so as to use him as a guide in our discussions. I question whether it will be of use for you to read him on your own. Were you to read it simply as though it were the word of God— inaccessible to our understanding, interpretation, and assimilation—then any book would be harmless for you to read. But you want to assimilate it all and take it by force; therefore the most useful words become harmful. What if you decided to assimilate the eight visions about which Peter of Damascus speaks? What if you were to hold on to even the first of these by force? Do you think I would praise you for such reading? One must know one's limits and hold to that word that is commensurate to one's limit, that of an unenlightened person. "*In the sweat of your face you shall eat thy bread.*"⁵ Is it right for us to dream about spiritual visions when we ourselves have not yet sweated in labor to obtain our daily bread, when the ground of our heart is constantly bringing forth weeds and tares? Lord, have mercy on us according to Thy great mercy! May the Lord cover you with His mercy! This is the wish and prayer for you of one who is sincerely devoted to you.

LETTER NO. 30   *March 31, 1873*

On Friday of the week of the Exaltation of the Cross, I attended Liturgy for the first time. I entered the church at the precise moment when they were singing: "Before Thy Cross we bow down, O Master." I immediately went and venerated the cross. After long and agonizing suffering, it was moving to venerate Christ's Cross, glorified by the Church, and to give praise to His uniquely redemptive suffering for us. Then I stood aside in my own place while the sisters went up to venerate it. All this time they continued to sing the verses: "Tasting from the Tree of salvation, we have been delivered from our sinful passions." My soul responded to these words with deep feeling. The Holy Cross was taken into the altar; I went into a side room of the church where I lay down for the remainder of the service. Then I became ill again . . . I bless all your effort and pray to the Lord that it be a saving path for you, leading you to an understanding of the power of God and of your own weakness, and to simplicity and faith.

LETTER NO. 31   *May 1, 1873*

Even though I am in the Crimea, why should you not write to me concerning your spiritual activity? I cannot promise always to reply to you, but having heard something from you, I shall not refrain from sharing something from myself and, if God deems it fit to enlighten me, then His word as well.

LETTER NO. 32   *May 30, 1873*

You asked my opinion of Father Archimandrite's decision to keep you in filth. I think this is too lofty a word for us. Because you are not ready to be trampled in filth, and have no faith in those who want to support you there, then in whom can one find enough selfless love to take you across the impassable lower depths in which not only is the mind humbled, but in which one loses the sense and taste of all that is good on earth? Alas, there is no other path—and therein is our calamity.

LETTER NO. 33   *June 3, 1873, Serbovo*

We spoke with our intimate ones today about the mind. There is nothing loftier and more valuable in a person. I confirmed my former opinion of this, for it is through the mind that we come to recognize all that is good and wonderful in the world. But now I am prepared to be deprived of even the mind, so long as I am not deprived of faith. The mind and emotions are tools of this age; they are perfected or weakened according to the age and life-path of each. Faith is the eye of the soul; it leads the soul into immortality and spiritual power. Yet faith itself, as a human feeling, is also nothing; but the Lord, to Whom the soul is brought by faith—He is the power and source of eternal life. In Him and through Him all is immortal, holy, and unchanging. What then, considering this, is the mind of man? Without God, without the Lord, it is mindless, it is as nothing.

LETTER NO. 34   *August 31, 1873, Theodosia*

I do not understand what your life is based on if a small distraction— such as changing a window in your cell, etc.—can fill you with such distress, emptiness, and listlessness. Go have a look and understand what the life of that great elder (I believe it was Sisoes) was based on, when he said: "If the heavens were to collide with the earth, my soul would not be afraid and my mind would not be separated from the remembrance of God." Where are you now, and upon what are you standing? Or consider him who said: *"Nor height, nor depth,"*[6] or: *"If I climb up into heaven, Thou art there; if I go down to hell, Thou art also there."*[7] Why do you lose all this on account of changing the window in your cell? Because you give only your mind to labor, and through it alone you wish to acquire and keep all, but are afraid to commit your heart to the service of the commandments of God because you fear it may be painful. This is what, filled with foreign perceptions, does not allow the mind to stay in the place you want it.

LETTER NO. 35   *September 25, 1873*

. . . but do not be quick to convince me that you have forgiven her already; that you have reconciled with her in your soul. I will not believe a brief spell of enthusiasm. What I speak of is a gift of God. Such peace is imperturbable; it is a love that carries all that is granted to the soul not only after the cleansing of prejudices but of the passions themselves. Our job is to recognize them within us and to eradicate them. To see this in ourselves, however, would be impossible if the Lord in His love for mankind did not reveal it to us through life's circumstances. A passion is recognized within the soul when the heart is oppressed, heavy, and eliciting indignation and despondency of spirit. Before the soul has sensed freedom from this, has not tasted of this peace and love, do not say or think that this prejudice is destroyed. The offense persists, masquerades in another form, and is, thereby, easily recognized. What brings sweetness is harder to perceive than that which brings bitterness. Thank the Lord that He grants us recognition of our biases and passions, freeing us from them through life's unpleasant experiences and especially through His Holy and life-giving Word.

LETTER No. 36   *December 19, 1873*

My spiritual condition is such that it requires a lot of work. This labor requires patience, then more patience, and even more patience so that the goal of patience is labor, and the goal of labor is endurance in patience. The labor should go no further; the patience should not stop any sooner. Without the Lord, neither one nor the other is attainable by the soul, so it labors and endures in its weakness and self-reproach.

LETTER No. 37   *February 26, 1874*

While fulfilling my requests, keep my will, desire, and thought in mind and not yours. As for your own thoughts, cast them away—for this will not be obedience but complete self-rule.

LETTER No. 38   *March 30, 1874*

I greet you on the eve of the feast of Holy Pascha. As yet I do not exclaim the joyful "Christ is risen!" but desire to venerate that tomb together with the myrrhbearers where through Christ all mankind found rest from slavery to sin and the devil. I am with you often in my thoughts. May the Lord preserve us all, as well as our Father Archimandrite. Please write to me more frequently and inform me of his health.

LETTER No. 39   *June 10, 1874*

Now I see what you are like! You labor for me intensely but censure yourself for performing obediences poorly, and are constantly concerned that I will be displeased. Any kind person would be surprised at your efforts and praise you for your humility, lack of trust in your own judgments, and labors. Perhaps I should do the same, but on the contrary, I am about to scold you. Why did you not wait and endure in silence? If I had truly found your obedience to be lacking I would have told you, and then would have been the time to make excuses and to say what was in your soul. As it is, you present so many excuses, you humbly confess and criticize yourself, that if in fact there was a mistake on your part, any kind human being with the exception of me would hasten to calm and comfort you. However, is this the monastic way? Where is the monastic endurance, silence, and acceptance of all that happens? Where is the path that allows all to occur with the Lord Himself at the helm? Self-love is evident in everything: it corrects itself, justifies itself, tears itself away far too early out of circumstances that are allowed to happen through the Lord's providence where one can learn self-reproach, humility, and denial of self if only it had patiently waited longer.

In this case, your embarrassment was unnecessary and if you had endured in silence you would have realized that it was from the enemy. Doubtless you would have felt intense bouts of disturbance, a darkening of the heart, leading to grumbling. These are all most obvious signs of the enemy's work. Your obedience was done so well with the help of the Lord that aside from thanking you I can say nothing further. You keep placing your hope in people's instructions; you value this greatly. Perhaps it would be so if we had spiritual instructors, but now, in our time, it seems that the Lord Himself instructs souls who seek salvation. He sends that which benefits us in good time. I was able to perceive your spiritual need when I spoke to you of fulfilling the commandments, but the Lord sends you circumstances and situations where you can labor. I ask you, does this come from man? One need only to labor lawfully with one's full strength, so that the spirit not only works but patiently restrains the thrusts of the mind, and through humility restrains all the movements of the heart, and always recognizes in all things the One Lord, Who is everything in all.

I am extremely busy, so I barely have the strength for everyday concerns. Life continues on its way. The other day, coming back from the brick warehouse through the orchard, I visited the schema-nun and shared with her the understanding I have recently discovered about the remembrance of death. As yet there is no time to talk to her about the remembrance of the Great Judgment. To you I will say that the memory of this is begun through God's commandments, the constant fulfillment of which becomes a permanent judgment seat, which the soul cannot walk away from or forget. I think that prayer will not be far from a heart that considers itself a constant transgressor, forever condemned for its impurity and hourly falling away from the right path. Enough has been said. . . .

LETTER NO. 40   *July 15, 1874*

. . . For this reason I did not tell you until now that I had been extremely comforted by the grace of God, which allowed me to be present at the blessing of the foundation of the church.

The image of the wonderworking icon of the Kazan Mother of God shining in the sunlight during the service was so joyfully bright that I could not help but pray to Her with contrition. Our Mitrophania was tonsured on the 13th, on the day of the Synaxis of Archangel Gabriel. She crucified herself with such selflessness and heartfelt humility that all present were touched and filled with fear, and I, covering her with my "mantia" experienced contrition and empathetic anguish.

LETTER NO. 41   *August 20, 1874*

. . . You asked about prayer. I cannot speak of it much because of inexperience. The prayer of faith, prayer with the consciousness of one's sinfulness, one's all-round weakness and inadequacy—this is the only prayer free of vanity of an individual who has not reached pure prayer. And to speak of pure prayer is inappropriate for me, as one who lacks it. It is the gift of God, and the crown of monastic life; it is possible with the action of the grace of God in the heart, or better said: it is the action of grace itself. The path to it is purity.

Through solitude, reading, and practice in prayer, purity of thoughts and feelings is not difficult to reach, but purity of heart is obtained only by many deaths; it is the removal of passions. Try to seclude yourself for a time, try to remove yourself from all cares and concerns. Give yourself over to prayer and you will see how your distracted thoughts calm down, how your shaken feelings subside, and you will begin to pray in a peaceful and attentive state. However, in the chest there is an inexplicable heaviness that weighs one down, pushes one down. It has no sudden thrusts, no desires, but lies like a stone on the heart, and produces darkness and tightness, which stands like a wall between the soul and the Lord. This wall can be destroyed only by the grace of God, commensurate with our determined battle against the passions, based upon God's commandments. As for us who live in the darkness of the passions, prayer with contrition, with faith in the saving Christ, is indispensable.

LETTER NO. 42   *March 6, 1875*

Remember that I told you I would like to make a beginning, but I did not tell you the beginning of what. "Weeds and thorns will the earth bring forth" and "you will eat bread by the sweat of your brow."[8] Such is the beginning. The earth of my heart is constantly giving birth to the weeds of the passions. It is the intent of the will to remove them with great toil, with constant attention to the heart, noticing them through the mind, acting upon them through the name of the Lord Jesus Christ.

LETTER NO. 43   *April 13, 1875*

Christ is risen!
    On the first day of Pascha I greet you with the Orthodox greeting and from my soul wish that in response your heart will fill with joy. Christ is risen! We do not experience joy to the fullest extent only because we have not died with Christ, we have not crucified our carnal will with Him and for the sake of Him. The resurrection of our own will, which comes alive at the completing of some sort of passionate sinful act, brings us more lively enjoyment. Let us weep then!

LETTER NO. 44   *May 8, 1875*

. . . I am sorry that your leg hurts. Sickness is a reminder of death, and one must prepare for it. I hear you asking: "How?" I think, by denying oneself the world, everything that constitutes its life and sweetness. Enough of working for the passions. The toil for them is finished, the accounts are settled. If in this work the soul has acquired, with God's help, some measure of patience, self-denial, humility, then she did not labor in vain as she served them. Yet this is not what is ultimately sought for; the soul must go further.

LETTER No. 45   *June 21, 1875*

I have read your account of S.'s dream and find that all that is written is true. The description of spirits and their action on the mind is absolutely correct. When a person lives for this world, he cannot fathom the extent to which his spirit is subject to another spirit; he cannot see this thoroughly because he acts as he pleases according to his own will. When the wall is removed with the onset of death, then the soul sees whose power it is under. The Spirit of God takes the righteous to the eternal habitations, enlightening and blessing them, making them divine. Those souls that were in contact with the devil will be possessed by him. This is why the Holy Fathers direct us to the true salvation not along a path of imaginary activity, but of real labor (*podvig*), both spiritual and bodily. With death the imagination is destroyed. It is destroyed even during life when—through a dream, an illness, fatigue, an interpretation, or various temptations— our desire to do good is weakened. At that hour and during the days of frailty, we see that our house was built not on a rock, but on the sand of fantasy. We do not create good thoughts and they do not stay in our mind; we do not invent good feelings and they do not abide in the heart, but are snatched away by the devil, who diverts our mind and heart to where we allow our inner evil disposition to take us. For this evil to be uprooted from our hearts we need special grace from the Holy Spirit. Labor in the commandments of the Lord is the only sure path to salvation; it heals the sinful essence itself, changes it to the likeness of God, and creates a situation in which all goodness is natural to the heart, and all truth is self-evident to the mind that has been reborn (through the grace of the Holy Spirit). I am unable to finish this letter in quite the way I had desired.

LETTER No. 46   *February 4, 1876*

During the Sunday reading we heard Vladyka's homily on the Lord's Prayer, "Our Father." All the sisters were very pleased and listened not only intently, but with love. Only I understood nothing, especially the words of the final petition: Thy will be done! How is it possible to know that holy will? And having accepted from the Lord an inkling of its meaning, how can I fulfill it, when the unbridled desire to follow my own sinful will, born of my fallen essence, drags me along. How can we sing the Lord's song in a strange land? For this reason, the only proper activity for the soul that finds itself on the banks of the River of Babylon is to "sit and weep." I wish you all that leads to salvation and spiritual progress.

LETTER No. 47   *February 6, 1876*

Yesterday we read the life of St Antony the Great. I liked his homily on the doing of good works very much. . . I am sending you an excerpt from it. It is so simple, yet so true. "Do not fear when you hear of the doing of virtuous works, do not let confusion enter your heart. It is not far from us, and does not develop outside of us; its work is within us and it is easy, if only we will try. The Greeks were willing to brave the seas and travel far in pursuit of an education alone, but we need not look far for the sake of the Kingdom of God, or cross an ocean in order to pursue good works. The Lord once said: *'The kingdom of God is within you.'*⁹ Thus, the doing of good is up to our will alone; for this reason it is part of us and develops within us. It grows in a soul whose rational powers work in conjunction with its essence. A soul reaches such a state when it becomes just as it was created: kind and absolutely righteous. Thus Joshua, Son of Nun, while teaching the people said: *'Incline your heart toward the Lord God of Israel.'*¹⁰ St John the Baptist says: *'Make His paths straight,'*¹¹ because in order for the soul to be good, its rational powers must be in harmony with its created essence. When the soul leaves this path and becomes incompatible with its essence, it is corrupted. Thus, this labor is not difficult. If we live according to how we were created, we are righteous. If we entertain evil thoughts, we are judged as corrupt. If righteousness were something that needed to be acquired outside ourselves, then, doubtless, it would be difficult to achieve. If it is within us, then let us guard ourselves from evil thoughts and retain our souls as a pledge received from Him, so that He can recognize it as His own creation, unaltered in any way. Let us strive not to allow irritability to reign within us, and that we not be overcome by lust, for it is written: *'For the wrath of man does not produce the righteousness of God.'*[12] *'Then, when desire has conceived, it gives birth to sin; and sin, when it is full-grown, brings forth death.'"* [13]

LETTER No. 48   *February 7, 1876*

Yesterday I read the homily of St Anthony the Great to one of the novices. I was telling her that these words so clearly and simply explain spiritual activity. She answered that, on the contrary, to her they seem unintelligible and complicated, because in herself she does not see and cannot find that natural righteousness that the Holy Father admonishes us to preserve. Moreover, she sees in herself only darkness, hardness of heart and desire for all which is evil; she feels an enlivening only when this evil desire is satisfied, or at least when she follows it; thereby, she considers evil more akin to her soul. See how persistent this corruption is in us, how much power the enemy has over our souls! And who can conquer him, or evade his power in order to see the path of light? The only One able to free us is He to Whom all things are possible. He said: Let there be light, and there was light. After this I wish to acknowledge no power, no strength, no influence over me but His almighty power, strength, and life-giving force.

LETTER No. 49   *February 9, 1876*

I cannot praise you for your letter to P. I see in it not only a blatant display of self-will, but also disrespect for my request . . . I asked you not to write anything, and you gave me your word that you would not act in any way regarding this without prior consultation with me. I hope that the deed itself will reprimand you and teach you not to act willfully. I am punished for entrusting a job I needed to do into the hands of a worldly person . . . I regret that I had to disappoint you at the start of my letter. Show some active obedience to my words; do not take this sorrow to heart but revert your feelings to renew a fervent desire to cut off your own will in your actions, words, and thoughts before me, before everyone with whom you chance to live with, meet, or converse with.

LETTER NO. 50   *February 14, 1876*

. . . When one loves one's neighbor for the sake of oneself, then it is fitting to strive for the fulfillment of one's own desires, one's own carnal will. If one loves him for his own sake, then one must fulfill his desires. If one loves one's neighbor for the sake of the Lord, it is necessary to strive to do God's will in all that pertains to him, and to walk blamelessly in His laws. Let us love our neighbor for the sake of the Lord. Renunciation is needed, not from the person, not from things, but from the passionate attachment to one and the other. Let us deny ourselves in order to give glory to the Lord Who saves us.

LETTER NO. 51   *February 20, 1876*

You sense a change in your spiritual state: glory be to God! The Word of God, accepted with faith, acts on its own. However, it acts only when the soul lives in utmost simplicity and humility, when through faith it genuinely gives itself over to God for guidance. The Lord sends circumstances and allows infirmities, sorrows, and deprivations [to visit the soul], causing a profound battle, profound spiritual exertion.

It is then that the Word of God, accepted through faith, guides the soul and gives it a true understanding of its condition, placing it in proper relationship to the circumstances at hand, and showing where and in whom it is to seek reliable support. From this the soul discovers that it is indeed, as the schema-nun says, the Godhead that saves it: through His word granting it true understanding; through circumstances leading it toward the proper action, and through abandonment prompting it to seek.

The sisters all send their greetings and consider you as one of us, despite the fact that you are a layman. May God have mercy upon both of us. I am not feeling too well, but illness of the body is not difficult to bear; it is harder to be sick in soul and to find no physician. A physician, however, is always near: the Physician who took upon Himself our sins and endured sufferings for our iniquities. He suffers for our sake, while we are healed by His wounds.

LETTER NO. 52   *March 16, 1876*

You ask: "How is it that we are to deny ourselves in order to give glory to the Lord, who saves us?" This is impossible to explain, but I believe that when the Lord grants the soul the joy of His salvation, then it understands that it acquired Him there where it lost itself; that its awareness of salvation came when it tasted the bitterness of death; and that it glorified the Lord Who saved it then when all its own schemes to save itself proved false, when it turned away from all of them as from vileness and lies. Lord, Thou Thyself art the salvation of my soul!

LETTER NO. 53   *March 27, 1876*

Today during Divine Liturgy the schema-nun stood near me, in her corner. After the service, I asked her to visit me in order to celebrate the day of the resurrection of Lazarus. During teatime I read to her from "The Ladder" (1st Homily, No. 6). Then we discussed the entire Canon of St Andrew of Crete, how it is formulated. At the beginning, man is depicted full of sin; all kinds of sins and vices are rooted deeply in him. From this knowledge of his sinfulness comes a sense of hopelessness and despondency. But Christ came to earth. He cleansed all manner of sin, uprooted evil in all its forms and manifestations. The soul finds courage in repentance; it seeks, as in Siloam, to cleanse the heart with tears; it finds the strength within itself to overcome carnal passions and vainglorious thoughts. Yet, in bringing forth these fruits of repentance, it realizes that it is not this sacrifice that is pleasing to God, and finally exclaims: "Do not require of me fruits worthy of repentance, for my strength is spent in me. Grant me ever a contrite heart and spiritual poverty, that I may offer these gifts to Thee as an acceptable sacrifice, O only Saviour." This verse, as I understand it, contains the very essence of the entire canon and the great labor of repentance. After this discussion and lunch, the eldress returned to her garden cell much comforted.

Write to me what "the symbol of victory" means to you. I will await a quick response to this question, and then I will tell you how I understand it. O Lord, grant that we may be reborn into newness of life in Christ Jesus!

LETTER NO. 54   *March 30, 1876*

Yesterday I received two of your letters, dated March 15 and 21. In one of them you describe your current state, which you term dullness of mind. You are troubled by the fact that when the soul finds itself in this condition, it has no power to deflect temptations, which cling to it through thoughts and feelings. The fact is that the soul never has the power to overcome passions; the Lord vanquishes them by the power of His grace. Yet you want to know how a soul should behave between that which you refer to as dullness of mind, when the mind ceases its activity, and despondency, when the inner spiritual feeling is likewise stifled. This can be a very difficult period for the soul. For one who is weak, a little diversion is permissible. For one who is stronger, it helps to keep oneself occupied with obediences, spiritual discussions, and, in general, physical labor. The Holy Fathers counseled the strongest one during this spiritual onslaught in this way: "Eat, drink, sleep, but do not leave your cell—and it will teach you everything."

Those who followed their advice called their cell "the Babylonian furnace." Where does this latter advice lead? To the discovery of the One Whom the three youths found in the Babylonian furnace. You will likely want to know, who is this strong one? He who has proper spiritual understanding. It is this that gives him the strength during times of temptation not to veer from the right path. One with less strength cannot expect this of himself, so he carries on with patience.

LETTER NO. 55   *August 18, 1876, Serbovo*

Once again, your trip to Voronezh did not come about. This leads one to think that it would bring your soul much benefit, and because of this so many obstacles have arisen. Your long-standing intent to venerate the relics of the great God-pleaser has still not met with success. You must strengthen your desire and resolve.

LETTER NO. 56   *August 20, 1876, Serbovo*

The Lord enjoins us to settle accounts with our adversary while we are still on the journey. (I don't remember exactly how it is expressed in the Gospel.) While we are still upon the path of life, we can pay these debts;

pay them by rejecting that which impedes our spiritual ascent, by rejecting all our material and emotional baggage. When the journey is over, there will be no possessions, no feelings to reject. All that will remain is poverty of soul and a wealth of spiritual strife, as with a debtor who had no time to pay his debt. A debtor suffers not only because his conscience bothers him, but even more because he is deprived of that which he supposed he had: all his possessions, his property, his freedom. Yes, one must pay off one's debt to one's adversary while on the way—pay it off through the renunciation of all things.

LETTER No. 57   *February 20, 1876*

. . . During this time there were many vexations and sorrows, as well as illnesses . . . If the internal difficulties (of the monastery) are troublesome, the external conflicts that come from contact with the world are even harder. Then one feels the helplessness of monasticism and the hatred of the world. Indeed, under these circumstances I often remember the words of the prophet David: It is better for me to fall into the hands of God than into the hands of wicked men. May the Lord preserve us from such a cross, which seemed unbearable even for the holy prophet.

LETTER No. 58   *September 20, 1876*

. . . Yesterday I visited the schema-nun and we discussed the fact that I am currently experiencing many sorrows. By bringing them about, the enemy is trying hard to overcome the soul, pushing it toward despondency, grumbling, lack of love for one's neighbor; while the Lord, by allowing these sorrows, wants to save the soul, giving it the opportunity through struggle to acquire courage, patience, spiritual wisdom, and, finally, humility, when these very sorrows overcome one's strength. Thus the soul stands between two paths, and whichever of these paths it is inclined to choose, that path will lead it to its goal.

LETTER No. 59   *October 13, 1876*

. . . You are indignant at P. P. for granting me crosses of sorrow. But you are mistaken. It is not P. but the Lord who is sending them to me.

I treasure them more than if they were gold, for they, more than any of our own efforts and toil, cleanse the pleasure-loving side of our soul. And often, partaking of the bitterness of sorrow, I say " . . . tasting from the Tree of salvation, we have been delivered from our sinful passions . . . " [Lenten Triodion, sticheron at the veneration of the Cross]. All circumstances are arranged by the almighty hand of God. He humbles and enriches, brings one down and lifts one up. And how good it is to come to know oneself and to feel oneself under His lofty right hand? Do not deliver us, Lord, into human hands through disbelief in Thy providence!

LETTER No. 60   *November 10, 1876*

The letter from A. P. disturbed you. This is understandable, but try to commit him to God's will. You can do this if you put your own will aside and stop pointing out what is best and most proper. It seems to me that he needs the freedom to live as he likes. If he is tired of his job in St Petersburg, would it not be better for him to take the position of a vice-governor somewhere in the country? Life there is less confining, more spacious in its own right. Your influence on him is strong, so be careful about giving him advice; it may be too severe for him and will oppress him. Love is good in that it gives liberty; it has no limits as to where it can go after its beloved. On the contrary, it can follow one even to hell itself. This is why love is so strong and more than once has snatched loved ones from the lowest depths of hell.

LETTER No. 61   *November 29, 1876*

You asked about the remembrance of death. It is good to have this, but within reason. When it encourages rejection of earthly things, compunction, humility, it is beneficial. But when it leads to despondency, the remembrance of death will lead not to salvation but to perdition. When one is despondent, it is more useful to think of God's mercy, His goodness, His gifts that He freely bestows upon us, the salvation that He grants to us through our life's circumstances and even through our failings. Everything is good in its own time, but when it comes at the wrong moment, even that which is most beneficial can serve as a detriment. Yet there is one labor appropriate at all times—the work of humbling one's spirit. This is best of all.

LETTER No. 62   *January 5, 1877*

While I was still in Serbovo, the newspapers informed us of the repose of His Eminence Leonid in Babaika. For this reason I was especially glad to receive your letters, which brought me a detailed account of these memorable days. How wondrous are the ways of God. I was struck with reverent wonder as I read about the circumstances of this event. The Lord granted you to witness part of a wondrous mystery: the passing into eternity of a God-loving hierarch, who had labored from childhood . . .

LETTER No. 63   *January 27, 1877*

Whenever something contrary to our will or unpleasant happens to us you always say, "It's God's allowance." I have never liked this expression; I find it inappropriate. Although I was not conscious of just why this was so, I never used this expression and never considered things that cause us displeasure and distress as God's allowance. I call this God's will. When our Lord Jesus Christ prayed in the Garden of Gethsemane before His impending Passion upon the Cross, He did not call this cup of suffering the allowance of God, but accepted it as the will of the Father. Similarly, in our own lives, all that is hard to bear is a manifestation of God's soul-saving will. We can consider the evil that we do the "allowance" of God. It can be said: God has allowed the enemy to act; He has allowed me to forget His commandments to give myself over to distractions, gluttony, luxury, and other sinful deeds. But by His will I was stricken with illness or another type of earthly misfortune that caused me to come to my senses and begin to distance myself from sin. See where God's allowance comes into play? There is evil where sin overtakes us, not where there are earthly or fleshly sorrows.

Yet we must not only accept the will of God, but do it. And in order for this to happen, we must, first of all, know what that holy will is. It is perceived by the soul when the Lord Himself reveals it. He does so when the soul walks before Him in righteousness. This righteousness consists mainly in the sincere intention to fulfill God's will, in the perfect readiness to renounce one's own will, and in the unwavering determination to accept all that the Lord sends without any debate or self-justification.

LETTER No. 64   *March 24, 1877*

Yesterday at the Liturgy, while listening to the chanting of the stich-era, I was saying to you in my mind: One can sell the Lord as did Judas for the cheapest earthly item, but one cannot take hold of Him by one's own power. Of His own will He came to save the harlot, sings the Holy Church. He Himself visits a soul, provided it does not sell Him in deed, feeling, or thought.

LETTER No. 65   *January 10, 1878*

As yet I have not written to you nor greeted you with the New Year. This is partly because I do not always respect the customs of the world and its constant changes. This would indeed be a new year of life if the soul came out of darkness and into light, from passions into dispassion. But what is new in our lives? Yesterday's passions and sins—are they not with us today, along with new ones, no different from the old.

LETTER No. 66   *October 28, 1878*

. . . It is obvious that you are rather despondent. Honestly, how can it be otherwise when a soul is left alone with its sins, passions, and weaknesses? How can it not grow despondent when it sees within itself nothing but evil and filth, and does not have the strength or discernment to leave the path of perdition? When, however, the soul turns to God, when it sees the depth of His compassion toward man-kind and the ways of His beneficent providence, when through faith in the ways of His providence—ineffable and soul-saving—it destroys all doubt within itself, then it feels strength, peace, and comfort. Then dark despondency leaves the soul and the stone of insensibility falls away.

Peace and joy are fruits of humility. This is the safe harbor wherein all the righteous ascetics, all who felt anguish within their soul, all who thirsted after salvation found solace. Do not be afraid to lose all for the sake of humility, to traverse the desert of despondency where the soul becomes bereft of everything, and unable to feel or move. From this state there is a quick path to humility through self-denial.

LETTER No. 67   *November 9, 1878*

My cheek was hurting all night. For this reason my hand is rested and I am able to write to you. . . . According to Fr Theodore and others, it would be better for me not to attend church at all. Each time I go out, my illness is exacerbated. And I would do that and pamper myself more if there was hope for the illness to pass, but since I am certain that it will remain with me for the rest of my life, I take the opportunity for an hour's or day's rest to go to church, perform some task, help out the sisters, or console someone by word or kind act. God only knows how many more hours like this I will have in this life.

In these days full of suffering, and through sleepless nights, I have grown to love using The Lord's Prayer, "Our Father." Only now have I begun to see its divine merit, its loftiness, its value for man, and for the Christian soul. For me it serves as a prayerful appeal to God, Who reigns everywhere, gives life to all, illumines all. It guides my spirit toward humility, my feelings toward moderation, my actions toward the paths of God, my efforts to the will of God. It directs all my being toward salvation. It carries me, enfolds me in truth. One needs nothing besides this divine guidance. Alone it is capable of guiding the soul onto the right path, of giving the soul all that is necessary for Christian perfection. But enough said. May you be well, and pray for me, a sinner.

LETTER No. 68   *February 3, 1879*

It's difficult for me to write, but I have taken up the pen anyway, to give a bit of news about myself and to tell you of yesterday's dream.

I dreamt that I was being shown a large painting of the Last Supper. A big table is set at which men are sitting to the right, women to the left, all dressed in clothing appropriate to the early Christian era. I look and am puzzled: Where is the Lord Jesus Christ? He is not depicted at the table, although His presence is palpable and His grace clearly illumines all present at the supper. I look more closely and see that at the right end of the table stands a deacon and at the left, a deaconess. Both are reading the Gospel. Seeing this, I bowed before the table with tears and exclaimed: "Lord! Now I have truly understood the Mystical Supper: all the saints commune of God's Word, perceive it spiritually, and are transfigured by it."

LETTER No. 69   *October 24, 1879*

I thought of you during Liturgy today. You always mention and have lately emphasized that you are in need of God's mercy. Yet this is not exact and is incomplete. We not only require God's mercy to forgive us our sins, to bear our weaknesses, to tolerate our iniquities, but in addition we need God's beneficence to cleanse us of our iniquities, to enlighten us to know His will, to strengthen us in our desire to do that which is pleasing to Him, to direct our will in fulfilling His commandments. When a soul discovers to what extent it requires these generosities of God and sees how much they benefit us, both in the external and internal aspects of our life, only then is a soul capable of praying to Him with a contrite and grateful heart, and only then will prayer be the vibrant word of the soul. The holy prophet David was led to the knowledge of the Lord as merciful and generous. This is why his prayer was full of gratitude, doxology, and contrition. Only the recognition of one's sinfulness brings one to search out God's mercy; only the awareness of one's powerlessness, helplessness, total weakness leads one to the perception of the most gracious Lord. I ask you to pray for me; I need the intercession of another soul before the Lord, Who is merciful and compassionate, but also all-just.

As I am accustomed to penetrate into the meaning of every deed and word, I often pondered over the tradition of asking forgiveness of everyone before the beginning of the fast. That day we ask forgiveness not only of those with whom we have had absolutely no contact and may not even have met, but even of those whom we do not know and have never even seen. Why does this custom exist—of asking forgiveness of everyone—when there is no logical point to it, and this all-inclusiveness only detracts from the real, fundamental purpose of this tradition? This is how I thought, and it troubled me. I was unable to make prostrations with the proper spiritual attitude and this grieved me. Only now has the true meaning of this been revealed to my soul.

We may not have personally done anything hurtful and we may not be guilty of any crime before everyone, but even if we were able to say with David: "Against Thee only have I sinned," then our sin indeed becomes a sin before many, and we are guilty not only before our brethren, but before all mankind. If our soul, in cooperation with God's grace, acquires a particular virtue, it becomes the property of all. He who is merciful has mercy upon all, he who is humble forgives all, he who is meek endures all, he who is experienced in battle with passions helps others, and so on. These virtues become the property of the whole world. They are spoken of, discussed among people for mutual benefit; even those far away hear of them. Thus, these virtues become examples to emulate and so provide strength and support. Our sins act in just the same way. Performed in the secret chambers of our heart—not only in word but even simply in thought—they pollute the heart, weaken it, and make it defective, feeble, dormant, blind, and deaf. Our sinfulness affects others; it affects the whole world. We do not give our neighbors that which they have a full right to expect and demand from us. We give them nothing: no love that carries and endures all, sacrifices all; no wisdom from our voice of experience; no example of endurance or good works. They likewise regard us with a lack of love, and our negative conversations about one another only serve to weaken and corrupt us. Thus, we are guilty before everyone and need to ask forgiveness of all. Here is yet another reason to deeply, deeply humble our heart.

LETTER NO. 70   *April 13, 1880*

Christ is risen! Today is the day of the resurrection of Lazarus—a day most appropriate for such a greeting. Once the soul fully perceives this event, that is, when the soul itself resurrects in Christ, it is able consciously to partake of the gifts of Christ's Resurrection. For us who sit in darkness and the shadow of death it is fitting simply to rejoice and thank God that He has given our human nature this ability, this great gift of being resurrected through Christ; to rejoice and thank God that there are and were chosen souls resurrected by Him from death to life, and to think humbly of ourselves.

LETTER NO. 71   *February 23, 1881*

Leonida has been home for ten days already. I am also pleased that she has returned, but I had grown accustomed to her absence, and there were times when I enjoyed my solitude . . . I am glad for the fast and the silence, though I ask myself: "What does this silence give me?" It is true that it gives rest to the body, which for my ailing constitution is very beneficial. Yet external silence and peace do not always bring peace of soul. On the contrary, frequently there arises a storm of passions within it. If during periods of distraction temperance is required, in times of solitude there is an even greater need for patience. Patience, when combined with spiritual discernment, faith of heart, and humbleness of spirit, is also a living power of the soul. It gives the soul endurance, develops into courage, and with time becomes not a passive feeling, but an active one. May the Lord strengthen you in patience, so necessary during the fast.

Letter No. 72   *July 1, 1881*

Thank you for your greeting on my birthday. By God's mercy I have reached the age of forty-eight. I see that my strength is waning and even my capabilities are decreasing. Spring, when all good seeds are sown, has long past. So has summer, when fruit ripens; now fall is passing, during which time the fruit is harvested. And what is there? Even if there is a small harvest, sown and cultivated by my reposed matushka through her labors and prayers, I am too slothful to gather it. Winter will come, and my soul will be dying of hunger. I became conscious of this the other day. One must compel oneself to prayer, and to everything that is good. I felt this so strongly that I shook off my laziness and forced myself to pray. It felt wonderful! But then laziness and indolence set in again. I am in such need of spiritual toil, of ascesis; it's absolutely essential! Pray for me, that the Lord send me strength to force myself toward such toil.

Letter No. 73   *December 14, 1881*

Spiritual peace is necessary not only to maintain a constant state of prayer, but even to fulfill one's prayer rule. If that spiritual peace is disturbed, prayer becomes either simply pronounced by the lips or accomplished with great effort by the mind; it can never be from the heart. Spiritual peace that belongs to those "pure in heart," is acquired—or better to say, sent by the Lord—after much toil and battle against the passions, after much self-denial. But we sinners, feeding on the crumbs from the tables of the rich, try to obtain peace at least during our prayer. Even for this, prolonged, arduous toil is necessary. During prayer we must completely cut off all thoughts; shun all feelings, all that belongs to the world around us; give everything over to the will of God; establish the heart firmly in peace; and possess unwavering hope in the power of God. With such a foundation in the heart, prayer is accomplished in peace. If, however, this condition is reached by our labors alone, and is not a gift of God's grace, then it happens that our inner peace is crushed and darkened by two "opposing" states: either coldness of heart or sensual joy, which replace confusion of thought and agitated feelings. Coldness of heart is such a monster that human powers are incapable of conquering it. In order to soften the heart, one must persist in the spiritual labor of love toward one's neighbor; one must have much compassion toward the weaknesses of others and forgiveness of these faults. Likewise, during prayer, with trust in the power of God, one must pray for one's neighbor, for the whole world, for "all people"; to "*save sinners, of whom I am chief.*"[14] The coldness will pass, only to be replaced by an irrational joy that disturbs inner feelings and one's inner peace. It is then that profound humility is required, even a temporary suspension of prayer because of one's unworthiness, and self-sacrificing service to one's neighbor, whether by word or deed. And it is only in the depths of humility and self-abasement that one finds the inner peace necessary for true prayer.

LETTER NO. 74   December 22, 1881

Blessed Jerome testified of himself: "My face was pale and my frame chilled with fasting; my flesh was as good as dead, and still my mind was burning with passions." He describes his spiritual toil for days and nights on end, his utter brokenness. And still the rebellious flesh continued to overcome his strength, and his soul succumbed to despondency. This persistence in spiritual toil, the unwavering steadfastness in it—these are the landmarks that are depicted in his icon. O Lord, grant for us to always endure in spiritual struggle—and whatever is above and beyond this is not up to us.

LETTER NO. 75   March 22, 1882

I have received and read the life of our Vladyka. I read it with much pleasure; it was very edifying and brought solace to my heart. Vladyka's own words are most precious, that is, what he says about himself. Another is able to speak of him only if he himself has risen to the level of understanding of Vladyka's works. The less said of him by others, the better. Very little has been told us about the author of "The Ladder," yet he will be the guide for all of monasticism—past, present, and future; and his image is so vivid and alive for every soul that is guided by him. I think that quite enough has been said about Vladyka for his current and future disciples. May this edition be printed and reprinted. To this I must add that it is essential that you gather all the materials, even small detailed accounts, write these all down in one notebook, and validate this with your signature. May this serve as a testament for Vladyka's closest followers. Perhaps in the future, these materials will find a broader application.

Brother Vasily M. writes that at the monastery they read Vladyka's biography, and he was amazed at its similarity with that of another person whom he knows well, especially in the way he was called to the path of spiritual life.

LETTER No. 76   *January 3, 1883*

The repose of my father, Michael Vasilievich, occurred on December 20. Although his passing away was very peaceful, for me it was so difficult that I felt as if I myself were dying. I arrived five days prior to his passing, and found him very weak and lying motionless in bed. He was not suffering, just gradually growing weaker. I did not leave him day or night. We conversed extensively. The final night he requested that I read the prayer "O Theotokos Virgin, rejoice." He remembered the works of Vladyka and that his best piece of writing is "On the Jesus Prayer." Whenever he was awake, my father constantly read the Jesus Prayer. During the final months, he received Holy Communion every two weeks and, in the final days, on the 15th and 20th—at 6 a.m. At 4 p.m. that day he peacefully reposed, as if in sleep. His burial took place December 23 at 2 p.m. His body, emaciated from prolonged fasting, was not quick to decompose. There were many people at the funeral, and no one's candle blew out. Everyone parted from him with tears, calling him a merciful father, a nurturer, and venerable one.

LETTER No. 77   *March 30, 1883*

You at least partially know how much I was attached to my dear father. If I fully respected anyone, loved anyone so fervently, adored anyone in my youth, it was him, my dear father, nurturer, friend, and spiritual guide. When I sat by his side those final days and nights, my heart overflowed with grief. I longed and was ready to drink the bitter cup of death instead of him. The Lord granted him a peaceful death. Nevertheless, his passing was difficult for me. I found solace and comfort through prayer for his soul. In the cell, all of us read the Psalter for his soul unceasingly for forty days. When I was reading the Psalter in my room on the eve of the fortieth day, I came to the 17th kathisma and felt a change in my soul. Although I read the words with my eyes and tongue, their meaning was conveyed to my soul by my father's soul. And this soul—which walked on this earth according to the commandments of the Lord and was rooted in His law, which had given itself over to His Word, which denied everything and its own self in order to follow the words of His lips—this soul, having left the earthly life with great hope and faith, communicated light and joy to my heart. That night I could not sleep from the fullness of happiness, and the fortieth day of his repose was for me a day of joy. That night many in Sebrovo saw him in their dreams, radiant, joyful, surrounded by light and convincing all not to grieve for him, for he is happy beyond all measure.[15]

LETTER No. 78   *March 21, 1884*

. . . It is not our imagination that should guide the spirit of our prayer, but that which constitutes the root of our life: our senses, all our thoughts, our spirit. Firstly, we must consider that which lives within us: a consciousness of our sinfulness, our inner acknowledgment of it in the spirit of repentance and contrition; and, secondly, that which we should live by: the commandments of God, written in our hearts at our creation, given to us in the Gospel and revealed to us in Christ. This constant battle with sin within our heart brings us to the knowledge of our utter sinfulness; this striving of the soul for the commandments of Christ brings it to the knowledge of its utter weakness, its powerlessness. Then the Jesus Prayer becomes the work of the heart, the breath of the soul, the spirit of life. In this state, it flows naturally, requiring no particular solitude or free time. It is acquired by the soul even when the soul is totally preoccupied; it acts in the heart even when the heart, strengthened by God's grace, is serving one's neighbor in self-sacrificing acts of love, whether by word or deed. However, we will stray from this course if our heart gives itself over and lives through the passions, or loses faith. In the first case, repentance and the cutting away of the passions will quickly return it to its former state. In the second case, a special grace of God will reestablish its faltering faith. I do not know if I was able to clearly explain to you the essence of this spiritual activity, but I know no other path. In solitude, or in setting aside free time for prayer, in deflecting inappropriate thoughts one should not run away from oneself or seek the Lord outside of one's own heart, or search externally for the exalted or for contrition. Within our heart, within its perceptions lies the reason for both our sinfulness and contrition. This activity brings one to a deep humility, to brokenness of spirit, to a sensation of spiritual warmth and compunction. Nothing stands in the way or detracts in this activity, and as the fathers relate, even hell itself is powerless to shake a believing and humble soul. Yet when we pray with a heart that is governed by our imagination, anything can serve as a distraction—even the wind, an overheard conversation, and similar things, not to mention our own weakness, which can divert us from the proper path to a point of no return. It is harmful to seek that which is external to us. If the Lord said that the Kingdom of God is within us, then it is there that we should seek it.

LETTER No. 79   *April 7, 1884*

Repentance, like prayer, should not be a product of our imagination, mere fantasy. True repentance is a gift of God; it is full of contrition. Our repentance, however, should be simply a consciousness, a certainty of our sinfulness, an awareness of the folly of self-reliance. This is what leads to faith. St Tikhon[16] writes well about this. We must read it together.

LETTER No. 80   *August 6, 1884, Kiev*

While listening to the heavenly chanting at the great Church of the Kiev Caves Lavra, I think of you, and how you called it a "tempestuous spirit."

This singing, so unlike anything else, comforts me greatly and fills my heart with an otherworldly feeling. You yourself know from experience how it speaks to the soul. I met the abbot of Optina Monastery, Archimandrite Juvenal Polovtsev. I like him very much, but we are not kindred spirits: our first conversation turned into an argument. I enjoy a little dispute when it is a matter of differing opinions, but when spirits differ, debate is pointless and it is better to keep silent.

LETTER NO. 81   *August 24, 1884, Ust'-Medveditsk*

. . . During this visit I diligently attended services at the Great Lavra Church. The singing at the Lavra, full of repentant contriteness and firm, unshakable, bold faith, awakened my slothful heart and brought it to contrition. It was sad to hear that those in charge do not understand this chanting and even criticize it.

The abbot invited me to visit him several times and we spent a number of hours in conversation. As a result, I understood that he is a spiritual man, but he is far from sharing a oneness of mind with us. I judge this from the fact that the longer we conversed, the further my soul retreated within itself. Even so, he is good monk and in his rightful place, as far as I can tell. As we parted the abbot said: "You are a shrewd one." He does not want to admit that we are striving toward the same goal, and that this striving even exists.

LETTER NO. 82   *November 12, 1884*

I had much to do these last few days. Along with the flurry of activity that comes with feast days and visitors, I wanted to strengthen the sisters preparing to be tonsured with a few words of inspiration—both individually and as a group. To some I suggested the curtailing of one's will and mind, which is possible only through the denial of one's desires. To others I suggested attention to one's thoughts, along with the continuous reading of the Jesus Prayer. To a third group, I recommended external ascetic activity, which leads to a pacifying of the carnal passions; to others, the unwavering adherence to Christ's commandments, which leads to the knowledge of one's weakness. To you, dear brother, I wish all of what I suggested to each of the sisters separately. May the Lord, through His grace, plant the seed of righteousness within the souls of those who draw near to Him and confirm their positive beginning, through the prayers of the most-holy Theotokos and all of our Holy Fathers and mothers in the Faith.

LETTER NO. 83   *November 20, 1884*

May you work out your salvation in Christ and remember us in your holy prayers. My closest sisters and I were filled with heartfelt joy when we heard that you had been tonsured to the riasophor. It is as though you have become closer to us, a relative. This spiritual relationship has always been so complete, that adding to it seems difficult. However, there is a correct measure for all things, and this measure has been fulfilled, or is about to be fulfilled.

You keep writing about hard-heartedness and sleepiness. I think that you are giving yourself too little rest. When you are overtired, you should not force yourself, you should not prod yourself into having a particular feeling. If you do not give your body rest and during times of exhaustion force yourself to pray or collect your thoughts, or to seek a state of repentance in your heart, you will never have peace of soul. On the contrary, you will have confusion of thought and heaviness of spirit. St Basil the Great says: "If rest is harmful to a young and healthy body, even more harm is brought to a sick and weak body by overwork." Do not be shy about giving yourself some respite and more hours of rest in order to gain some hours or even a few minutes of spiritual vitality, a fresh outlook, and clear thought. Otherwise, one can fall into despondency. The Lord wants so little of us, just a humble spirit, while He gives us everything through His grace.

LETTER NO. 84   *December 8, 1884*

Mud, rain. The Don River has not frozen over yet, but already there is no possibility of crossing. Therefore, no one visits us, and the weather is keeping me within these four walls. I am very content with my solitude, though I do not always use it to my advantage. I love long winter evenings. Sometimes I gather my closest sisters together for a reading, and

I give my interpretation. This is not the same type of reading at which you were present in the past. Now only the closest ones gather and there is more freedom in our discussions. After one such reading Veronica said to me: "I only took in but a single thought of what you told us, and it is sufficient for me. You said that when one gets carried away by something it is good to remember the hour of death, for at that point nothing will be necessary; everything on this earth will stay and only the soul with its deeds will go forth alone. This thought leads me to prayer and gives liberty to my spirit." Through teaching the sisters I learn from them myself. We read mostly from *The Philokalia*. I have not read this book in a long time. Much of its content is revealed to my understanding now, whereas it was previously closed to me, although even now much remains hidden.

LETTER NO. 85   *February 7, 1885*

I thank you for the news about the cross. Everyone is very glad. As am I. Honor is better than dishonor, and my soul is still far from being able to view equally the one and the other. But I must admit: ambition is not my greatest passion; there are others who are stronger. I see that in myself pride is stronger than ambition. And how is it that these opposing passions can coexist in one heart? The one who craftily sows these tares knows, as does the one who entertains them unnaturally in his heart.

I have finished the account of Schema-nun Ardaliona. I wrote with no regard for rules and laws of composition. Once having decided that it will not be published—at least in its present form, I was not bashful. I spoke a lot about myself, relating many of matushka's discussions with me. I also wrote of Schema-nun Pafnutia, where mentioning Matushka Ardaliona and myself likewise became necessary. We were all pleased with this written work. For us it resurrected the time we spent with matushka; all she said, all she did in giving us guidance.

LETTER NO. 86   *March 5, 1885*

You have requested to read my notes about matushka Schema-nun Ardaliona. I myself want you to read them very much, but I should like first to rewrite them, for they are written in a barely legible scrawl, with so many corrections and marginal notes, that they are hard to decipher. Just yesterday I received them back from Pravdin. I will send them to you when I have rewritten them.

Letter No. 87   *December 1, 1885*

What can I tell you of myself? It is best to keep silent. I am beginning to understand that silence is more fruitful than any word. To maintain silence in word, thought, and feeling—such a silence is desirable, for what one says, thinks, and feels: all is sin, passion. "Let all mortal flesh keep silence." My sinful soul is far from such silence, but sometimes there comes a keen desire for it, when the soul is burdened by vanity, when it loses the taste for all things earthly, transient, as though it sees the transitory nature of our mortal flesh. Then it desires to keep silent.

Letter No. 88   *December 1, 1885*

We all need to keep death before our eyes, for it is always with us, as each day that passes, each hour, each minute gone by, has already died for us—forever. We live in death, we are dying every minute and our sinful deeds are leading us toward everlasting death. But this vale of tears and death must be traversed with faith until the Lord Himself finds that the fruit is ripe and it is time to harvest it.

Letter No. 89   *November 26, 1885*

I can say about myself that I am healthy; I attend church daily, I fulfill my obedience at home, I read, I write . . . But that is not enough for you. You want to know how my soul is faring. It lives in sins; moreover, in insensibility of its sinfulness. Once in a while the eyes of the soul are opened and it sees its blindness and sinfulness, and that is frightening. Yet what does it do to shed its blindness, to retain that fear in the heart so that this knowledge of its own sinfulness would lead it to the rejection of its sin-loving will, of its false mind-set? Herein lies the soul's misfortune: it is burdened by the need to labor on the inner man and it seeks respite in the distraction of the mind, in the restlessness of feelings. Please pray that the Lord direct my soul toward repentance.

LETTER No. 90   *February 20, 1890*

I keep thinking that your illness is not fatal . . . I hope that you will recover. It is difficult for me to think that you will pass on to the future life and that I will never see you again. I never ask the Lord for anything and always leave all things to His providence. I ask that all be done according to His good and salvific "soul-saving" will. Meanwhile, I am fervently entreating the Queen of Heaven that she support you, so that I can see you again on this earth. If the Lord blesses us to remain alive until spring, wait for me. Gather your strength and recover; strengthen yourself in body and soul. Strengthen your spirit through faith. Do not frighten yourself with images of impending death and how you will answer at the judgment. Do not carry in your soul the fear of death. Such fear is beneficial to our salvation when we are living a worldly life, in passions and carnal desires. When, however, our life nears its end, when we look to the world beyond, this fear can become a great temptation. Regard it as such. Look upon the coming transition with faith and hope, strengthen your spirit with the hope of God's promise. Place all your hope in what He does for us, in His mercy, in His love for man. Man indeed is sinful, but belongs to Him alone. You yourself have nothing. Your soul is dead; it has no memory of God. But be assured of His ability to save. Chase away fear and hopelessness. A believing soul, a soul dedicated to His will, will not perish. When we first met, you told me that you have nothing with which to save your soul, and that you wish only one thing; that you may live in Vladyka's monastery like a little dog. I remember this very clearly. And so it will be. In Vladyka Ignatius's heavenly abode there is a light-filled place prepared for you. Believe this and rejoice. If despondency or fear come, chase them away and think about the transition to the life beyond the grave with hope and joy. And to those who lie in wait for your soul at the gates to carry it away, say boldly: You have no part with me; I am the obedient novice of my fathers, who will answer for me before my Lord God. Amen.

LETTER No. 91   *March 1, 1890*

I am afraid that you are burdening yourself with heavy lenten food. Forget that this is lent and eat nonlenten food, nutritious and light. One can forget about the difference between fasting and nonfasting days when one believes that this is given to us by the Church as a restraining bridle for a healthy body. You, however, have been granted illness and the infirmity of old age . . . Most important, I entreat you, do not aggravate your spirit. May it be peaceful in all circumstances, as a child entrusted into the arms of the Saving Lord; and strengthened, as a grown man girded about with faith in the hope of the mercy of Our Redeemer. "What are our sins in the face of the mercy of God?" asks Dmitri of Rostov. "Like a cobweb against a mighty wind." Let us rejoice in our Lord and Saviour. Let us be peaceful and of good cheer. Unfathomable are the paths of God whereby we find salvation.

LETTER No. 92   *March 8, 1890*

Today is the fortieth day of the repose of our dear friend Archimandrite Justin. Through the prayers of Vladyka Ignatius may the Lord grant him eternal rest with the saints! We prayed for the repose of his soul and prepared a commemorative meal. I wept through the entire panikhida. I recalled him as if he were still alive, his whole life: from the age of nine living within the walls of a monastery as in the Babylonian furnace; as a young abbot, then a confessor and martyr. Another thing I will say to you alone: the spiritual path that is founded upon the renunciation of self-will is always without honor. The Lord does not give him honor on this earth and He does not confirm his righteousness even through the manner of his repose. May He alone be our truth and defense, our holiness and sanctification. Abide in peace within this faith and hope.

LETTER No. 93   *August 2, 1890*

Glory to God for all things! In your current condition, because of the frailty of your elderly state, the most important thing for you is to be at peace with all those around you and to feel peace within your own soul. I was comforted to hear that you have become close to Father Elijah. I hope that he will bring you comfort. I am touched by the love with which you treat Fr P. and your condescension toward Fr M. Do not think that I accuse them of anything or judge them. I cannot pronounce judgment on anyone. All is in the hands of God, and those all-powerful and merciful hands desire that all men be saved and freely give this salvation to all. I only say that our path is the path of sinners, such as we truly are. We must be humble and not stray from this path of repentance, nor put on a mask of righteousness. We are sinners and should not seek justification, but should hope and believe that our justification is Christ. We must not be ashamed of our brothers and fathers if their life seems shameful and their death dishonorable. It is better for us to emulate their faith and humility and to commit ourselves to the Lord who saves us.

PART 3

Letters to Other Individuals

Following, dear reader, please find another thirty-eight of her letters written to various other individuals. Unfortunately, the original text gives little to no biographical details of the recipients of Abbess Arsenia's correspondence.

An early letter of Abbess Arsenia (then novice Anna) to her sister, Agrathena Mihailovna Merzhanova.

To Agrathena Mihailovna Merzhanova   *December 17, 1851*

I thank you for your letter and for your love for me, the unworthy one. I am glad that your health is improving. May the Lord grant you a full recovery, my kind sister. Yet even an illness can sometimes be beneficial for us. The merciful Lord chastises us here with temporary suffering in order to save us from eternal torments. It is so comforting to know that we are strangers here on earth and that our homeland is in heaven! And how desirable is this homeland! Lord, deprive me not of Thy heavenly good things. . . . deliver me from eternal torments. Yet if the soul is entirely filled with Divine love, it does not fear Gehenna, for even there it will be united to the Sweetest Jesus and will love Him. Lord, grant that I may love Thee with the same love with which Thou hast loved me! Thou camest down to earth for me, when my soul could have ascended to heaven for Thee!

I greet you with the feast of the Nativity of Christ and entreat the newly born Lord that He renew all the virtues within your soul and bring you to a measure of perfection.

To Schema-nun Pafnutia from
the City of Feodosiya   *August 5, 1873*

We attended liturgy yesterday and I was greatly comforted by the Word
of God. It is always dear and powerful for me; it both nourishes and
enlightens the soul. During the communion of the clergy the choir sang:

> Having risen from the tomb and having burst the bonds of hades,
> Thou hast destroyed the sentence of death, O Lord, delivering all
> from the snares of the enemy. Manifesting Thyself to thine Apostles,
> Thou hast sent them forth to preach; and through them has granted
> Thy peace to the world, O Thou Who alone art plenteous in mercy.

These words seemed alive to me, and I saw their power within the
context of human existence and spiritual life. Man lives an earthly life,
wherein all is mortal and transient. Circumstances change, human feelings are inconstant. By confining oneself to such earthly conditions and
emotions, if a person lives only in the realm of circumstances and feelings, he is constantly partaking of death; everything in his life is dying;
he finds himself under sentence of this death.

When, however, a person in this transient, mutable life seeks the Lord;
when each circumstance points him toward the knowledge of the Lord;
when each feeling, directed according to God's commandments, brings
him closer to the contemplation of the Lord (Whose likeness is restored
in a pure heart); when the Lord is resurrected within the soul—then the
sentence of death is destroyed. Here we see that earthly conditions and
sensibilities are capable of bringing a man into a state of immortality,
and that partaking of them did not bring death, but rather life. When,
however, a man lives by earthly things alone, the enemy is able to use
all earthly situations to lay his snares for that person. If, on the other
hand, what is earthly is transformed for that person into immortality,
if it brings a person to know the Lord in these temporal conditions and
to union with Him in spirit, then the snares of the enemy are destroyed.
The Lord, perceived through earthly life then Himself becomes salvation from the perdition that was prepared by the enemy, from the nets
that held the deadly poison. This is all perceived within the spirit, a direct
personal experience of the soul, wherein it finds a confirmation of God's

Word. May the Lord grant that we not simply read and glorify His Holy Word with our lips, but emulate Him in our lives.

To LYDIA P. V.   *November 15, 1870*

. . . I am always glad to hear of someone's desire for the monastic life. If a well-educated and intelligent person dedicates himself to this life, I rejoice all the more. However, it is important to know what prompts the person to choose this life, what aim he has in mind in making this choice. His aim sets the direction and character of his subsequent life and activity and is therefore of primary importance. You write that you wish to enter a monastery because of all the misery you see around you. I do not understand this. If you are looking only at the outward side of life, and want to escape earthly sorrow and to find solace in the quiet life of a monastery, you are making a mistake. A monastery has its own tribulations, perhaps even more grievous than those found in the world. If within your spirit you have felt the vanity of worldly life, if you do not find satisfaction in it and are looking for the fullness of spiritual life, if you desire to live for the sake of eternity, for God, you have the proper aspiration. However, in making this decision, you must prepare yourself for all manner of trials, both spiritual and physical. Much is demanded of a person who wishes to be saved. The walls of a monastery, the black attire and all of the external labors of monastic life mean nothing without the inner ascetic struggle, which is the true goal of monastic life. It requires a complete regeneration of one's entire being, the renunciation of everything earthly, the obliteration of all that is one's own—human reasoning, human feelings—in order to come alive for God and in God. As far as a man is removed from God, as great as the chasm that separates him from God, so great is the labor of reuniting with God. Not only is the path difficult, for many it is impossible, and it does not open itself to all. Not everyone finds it, not everyone seeks it—or even desires it. One who genuinely yearns for it, searches and finds it must be called to this path by the Lord Himself. The soul feels this calling when it finds no satisfaction in earthly pursuits, when it constantly feels unfulfilled and seeks within itself the perception of immortality which leads to eternal life, which draws one closer to the eternal Lord. The soul cannot resist this calling, for it grows obedient and constantly seeks the inner life, communion with the Lord, until it finally finds the path that leads to its goal. Even then it continues to till the soil of its heart and travels on and on, despite the fact that the path it has chosen grows increasingly difficult and requires more and more self-denial. And it remains within these straits to the end of its days, until God wills for it to be called to eternal life. If the person does not wish to undertake this inner spiritual toil, if he does not seek this path, he ought not enter a monastery. This is a school of spiritual life, and one goes there in order to educate one's spirit, to find instructors and all the resources necessary to traverse this spiritual arena.

Think this through carefully, prepare yourself as best you can, and only then make your decision. Familiarize yourself with the requirements for an inner spiritual life and listen carefully to your spirit: is it capable of subjecting itself to this, is it inclined toward this new calling? You can familiarize yourself with this by reading "The Ladder" of St John Climacus and the fourth volume of the works of Bishop Ignatius (Brianchaninov).

* * *

The next set is written to a certain person identified only as V. I. I. We do know the four-year period when the letters were written: Letters to V. I. I., 1885–1889.

Letter No. 1 to V. I. I.

Do not try so hard to know God's will so as not to mistake for it the ardor of your own heart. We must realize and deeply acknowledge that our heart is so damaged, so darkened by sin; our life is so entangled with our shortcomings, so disfigured by the self-willed strivings of our sin-loving heart, that we are not only incapable of knowing or fulfilling God's will, we do not even allow it to act within us, to direct our lives. The prophet says: "*Unto the saints that are in His land hath the Lord made wonderful all His desires in them.*"[1] Do you see? It is in holy hearts, and only through them, that the Lord fulfills His holy will, for they present no obstacles, no resistance. A sinner, on the other hand, who lives by his passions, constantly opposes God's will. And it is good if he accepts those trials that God allows to befall him, if he humbles himself beneath the hand of God. Such humble submission to whatever God allows is a sign of a repentant sinner. In living a sinful life, we accumulate a great deal of unrighteousness; with our sins we cause others to stumble, and we may be responsible for their perdition. A repentant sinner recognizes that it is difficult to reconcile himself with his past; that he needs to redeem himself through great ascetic toil and struggle. He must save not only himself but everything and everyone around him, to lead them to the path of truth and righteousness. This is a difficult and lengthy endeavor, but it is noble and true. And if it is true, then it is possible with the help of God's grace. Yes, this is the only true way. We must bring forth fruits worthy of repentance; we must labor where we have sinned, rise up where we have fallen, fix that which we have destroyed, and save that which we have lost through carelessness or through our own passions. Salvation is possible in all places and all occupations. We need not seek it outside of ourselves, for all can be found within our own soul, both paradise and hell. If within it we find hell, therein can we also—by God's grace and by working on ourselves—find paradise. There is one condition under which it is permitted to run away and completely change one's life. That is when our own weakness has reached its uttermost limit, when the soul has no strength not only to struggle but even to endure, when this is accompanied by physical infirmity as well. In such case we will not sin if we run away from such an intolerable situation.

Letter No. 2 to V. I. I.

You have resolved to forsake everything and to follow Christ. This is commendable. But where do you find the path to Him? You expected to find it through theological studies at seminary, but to no avail. The education there simply explains the letter of the law, but not its spirit. You desired the priesthood, monasticism. This is good. But I am afraid that you will scarcely have begun when you notice that you have changed location and attire, but your life—internally and even externally—has remained the same. What is necessary is self-denial and conformity to God's word under the tutelage and direction of a holy (spiritual) person. The question is, where do you find him? It is possible, if one searches.

For this reason I advised you not to rush with your decision so as not to make a deliberate move and then regret it when you find yourself dissatisfied with what you have chosen. I suggest that you take some time off and go visit some Russian monasteries where there are elders with whom you could speak and from whom you could receive some direction for your life.

Letter No. 3 to V. I. I.

Just as virtues are bound together in an indissoluble chain, so too are vices. They are closely related and it is hard, impossible really, to determine where one begins and the other ends. If the acknowledgment of one's weakness and sinfulness is the beginning of faith, it is also the beginning of one's salvation. If without faith it is impossible to do God's will and follow His commandments, so it is inconceivable to acknowledge one's weakness unless one labors to fulfill God's holy laws. Only by submitting one's will to the will of God, by resolving to walk in the way of His commandments and heading in this direction can the soul become aware of its own weakness, its passions, and the depth of its sinfulness. Instead of the love for one's neighbor that we are called to have, the soul will find in the heart only self-love; instead of the perception of God's will, it will find in the mind only self-opinion, foolishness. And how much infirmity of soul and utter lack of willpower comes along with this! Only then will it begin to seek help from heaven, for through experience it will be convinced that without the help of God it is altogether powerless. Then with animated faith will it seek Him who lives and acts within the world. With the cooperation of God's grace the soul will be able to fulfill God's life-giving commandments, thereby receiving enlightenment and sanctification. This is the stature and the crown attained by the saints. But it is the labor of a lifetime. Do not think to achieve this in a hurry: to reach that which is beyond the ability of man without the help of the grace of God. Our duty is simply to labor with humility and faith. During this effort the soul will be swayed by various emotions, both pleasant and unpleasant; it will alternately be joyful and despondent; it will become distracted. But this should not trouble us. We must steadfastly preserve determination to submit our will to the will of God and to give our mind over to faith. This is why I have told you to pay more attention to the will than to the feelings of the heart; to the inclination of the mind than to the thoughts themselves.

LETTER NO. 4 TO V. I. I.

You can keep the first volume of Bishop Ignatius Brianchaninov; later I can give you another one. I want to give you some advice regarding this reading. The book you are reading is called *Ascetic Experiences*, and it was written by a monk ascetic. In it, as in all the works of Bishop Ignatius, is advice given to ascetics, to those who have renounced the world. Although all Christians should follow the path of Christ's commandments, rejecting their sinful passions, there is a difference in their spiritual endeavors, in their lifestyle, if one can express it in this way. Recluse, novice, or layman—each can achieve the renunciation of self-will. But the path to this goal will be different for each. The recluse discerns God's will and submits to it his own will, in light of the word of God; the novice achieves the same through submitting to the will of a spiritual father, while the layman accomplishes this through life's circumstances. Purity of heart is possible for all three, but the first achieves it through constant prayer, the second through obedience and confession of his thoughts, and the third through honest fulfillment of his occupational responsibilities and familial duties. All reach the same goal, but through different means. So it should be in all matters of life. I have indicated the main aspects, but there is one thing that I particularly want to say to you: I fear that you might be unduly inclined toward asceticism. Monasticism is no more than an external form, and, no matter how exalted, it should not be the zenith of our strivings. "*Desire the best gifts*,"[2] says the apostle. All spiritual treasure is hidden within Christ's commandments: to love God above all, and one's neighbor as oneself. How greatly we must strive to reject our passions in order to come to love God above all earthly things, more than ourselves! How much we need to battle with ourselves in order to grow to love our neighbors as ourselves! Within these two commandments lies all purity and holiness of the soul.

Remember the words of Matushka Ardaliona. She said that one must also learn how to love oneself. Yes, and this requires great effort.

For example, a man can be unfair to himself and demand of himself the impossible. Expecting to overcome his passions he becomes despondent, frustrated, and angered as he sees that the very passions he has chosen to battle with have taken hold and overcome him. Is such self-contempt justified? No. A man cannot conquer his passions on his own; they are overcome by the power of God. This power is contained in His commandments. When with God's help man assimilates them, when they begin to rule within his heart, then sin and passions weaken their activity in the heart and cease altogether. We must constantly renew our determination to live by Christ's commandments, we must pray for His help, we must humble ourselves when we stray, we must accept the fact that we are weak and not become exasperated with ourselves. We are incapable of conquering, so why demand of ourselves that which the Lord alone can give? Why bemoan the fact that we are unable to rise above ourselves? Such demands for spiritual perfection reveal our pride. Let us wait for all things from the One Lord and use our failures and sinfulness to fervently humble ourselves. Passions can stubbornly lodge themselves in our hearts, and act as though they are in charge, contrary to our will. The Lord allows them to torment us so that we might come to know the full extent of our weakness and to humble our hearts, so that we would seek strength in our One Mighty and One Holy God. I write these words in answer to your complaints that you sometimes become cross. Do not lament but humble yourself each time and determine to be patient, and in patience fulfill God's will and His holy commandments. Once you come to the knowledge of your own weaknesses, you will come to understand the weaknesses of your neighbor.

If you cannot conquer your own passions (when by God's mercy you are even able to see them), despite the fact that you desire to overcome them and strive to do so, how can you demand from your neighbor that which lies beyond his strength? Become aware of this weakness that is common to us all, and try to forgive your neighbor, to be at peace with him, and to bear with his shortcomings.

Letter No. 5 to V. I. I.

In your letter dated May 19, you expressed fear that our correspondence may end. No, I am not even thinking of stopping it while you are still in need of my letters, as long as they bring you benefit and comfort; and while the Lord continues to endure my own sinfulness by giving me the ability to understand His Holy Word. However, a spiritual conversation and spiritual guidance are two different things. I generally avoid guiding anyone but the sisters who have been placed under my care. God's own Word should be your guide. Is it not enough for me to occasionally clarify God's Word for you? Let the process stay the same as it has been up until now. If you find yourself a better guide, that will be fine, but if not, let us help each other to find God's way—as long as we do not lose the steadfastness and desire to strive for the goal, to work hard, to believe that the Lord will lead us there and to expect this from Him alone. You may be wondering, what is this goal and which path leads to it? The goal of human existence is to communicate with God; therein lies the salvation of our souls, their everlasting blessedness. The path is to follow His commandments, to submit to His will, which is revealed to us through our life's circumstances. The labor is the cleansing of our heart of passions. Humility is what brings one to faith, to the acceptance of God's grace, without which nothing good or holy can happen within us. Many noble individuals are able to rise above the letter of the law, but even they do not always see the need and advantage in this. The letter of the law has destroyed much goodness and holiness in us, in our Christian community. We must strive for the letter of the law to come alive within us, in order that it not destroy us but rather give us the life of the spirit—or at least point us in the general direction of that life.

Letter No. 6 to V. I. I.

I want to say a few words about the Gospel commandments. The Lord Himself indicated the two most important ones, which encompass all the others: love of God and love of neighbor. Yet there are other commandments, which He gave in the Beatitudes when He said: Blessed are the poor in spirit, etc. Those commandments identify the qualities of soul and heart that need to be developed. Only then does it become possible to fulfill the two most fundamental commandments. Begin with the first one: to be poor in spirit requires us to destroy our self-centeredness and self-will, to see the total powerlessness of our soul, all its weakness and sinfulness. If a person sees, knows, and feels this way, he will inevitably come to faith, to the conclusion that in God and in Him alone lies all his strength, his purity of soul, his salvation. This faith is already a door to the Heavenly Kingdom, not only to that which is to be the eternal abode of holy souls, but to the kingdom that is within us. Such poverty in spirit is truly blessed because when a person comes to see the utter powerlessness of his soul, its filth and lack of anything good, he begins to lose faith in himself, to stop depending upon himself.

Therein lies the beginning of faith and hope in God, for it is in losing himself that a man finds God. It is difficult and very bitter to find oneself in this wretched state of helplessness. It seems that one is perishing, that there is no salvation, no help from anywhere. Yet this needs to be experienced in order to come to faith. We must come to realize this not only in our minds: our whole being must acknowledge its weakness—to live in it—only then will we come to a living faith in God. We will see Him acting in all things—once we stop acting on our own, through our self-will. We will see Him reign over all when we cease trusting our own judgments, our own self-reliance.

You ask, were Schema-nun Ardaliona and Bishop Ignatius acquainted? No, they did not even know of one another's existence. I did not know Vladyka either. It was only in 1867 that I was able to obtain his writings. They were published in 1865. Matushka Ardaliona reposed in 1864. When I read the first volume I was amazed at the similarity of our spiritual journeys. By that time, my spiritual outlook had been established and I had spiritual children. When they read Bishop Ignatius, they likewise noted the similarity of our spiritual concepts. This was the case among Vladyka Ignatius's spiritual children as well, whom I visited in 1867. I possessed only the first volume at the time . . . But I must tell you that it is impossible to grasp these spiritual concepts through reading alone—one must live by them. I want to give you one obedience: learn by heart the twenty-four prayers of St John Chrysostom: "Lord, accept me in repentance, Lord, forsake me not, etc." It is good that you have passions. The Holy Fathers say that if there were no passions, there would be no crowns for the victors for those who conquer them. And how beautiful are these crowns! . . .

LETTER No. 7 TO V. I. I.

You seek to understand everything with your mind and only then begin to properly work on your heart. This cannot be granted to human beings. We are unable to properly assess our condition before we are cleansed of sin. The mind itself is darkened. To come to an awareness of your sinfulness, you should begin by realizing that you do not understand yourself, that you have no insight. It is sin that has dimmed the spiritual eye, and in this blindness you should acknowledge your sinfulness, your weakness. And so it should be in everything. Now is the time to repent, to acknowledge sinfulness. Do not wait for it to reveal itself to your mind, but learn to see it from the inadequacy of the mind itself, in the powerlessness of your will, in the inconstancy of the heart.

LETTER No. 8 TO V. I. I.

In several letters you ask about the Gospel commandments. This question shows that you are willing to submit yourself to these laws; that you have decided to take on the struggle to live by them. May God help you! But why do you ask me about this? Open up the Gospel; read it, delve into that which the Lord taught His disciples and you will understand what commandments He gave to His followers. He taught them renunciation of all things, particularly of the self, even to the point of renouncing one's own soul. Such renunciation is absolutely essential, because within our heart there is so much filth, so many passions that are contrary to the spirit of Christ. Without renouncing them communion with Christ is impossible. This self-denial is possible only when there is a purpose, a goal for which we sacrifice ourselves and deny our passions. This goal is love for one's neighbor. In order to fulfill our duty of love toward our neighbor, we must leave our self behind and renounce our own soul. The Lord showed us both in word and deed and by His own example how to walk the path of such love. He taught us to forgive our enemies, to have mercy on the weak, not to judge sinners, to sacrifice ourselves for the benefit of others. This commandment of love toward our neighbor is impossible to fulfill without cutting off our love for worldly pleasures. Self-denial and a willingness to give all to one's neighbor is possible only when we seek eternal life, when we try to love the One Eternal Good, the One Absolute Perfection: God. And herein lies the most important and first commandment of Christ: to love God with all our heart, mind, and strength. The Lord indicated the perfection of such a path in just a few words, but to fulfill these words, to master them, takes more than a lifetime. But who am I? To understand oneself properly, to see all the grime of one's own soul, its passionate character, its feebleness—this is the goal of an entire lifetime for those who seek salvation. Salvation, I say—but what are we to be saved from? We are saved from the state of perdition in which we presently find ourselves. Therefore, it is essential to determine what sort of precipitous condition this is. It is our common plight: the perdition that we ourselves create from our passions and sins; a perdition that we do not see within ourselves, nor even suspect that it is there. Meanwhile, that which lives within us prevents us from following Christ. This happens in spite of our resolve, in spite of our desire to change. So it is necessary, first of all, to cleanse the inside of the cup,[3] our inner vessel, from which, in the words of Christ, come fornication, murder, theft, and all manner of passions and sins.[4] This is why, when speaking to you, I am constantly pointing out the passions of the soul. I want you to comprehend the utter defilement of the human heart, your complete weakness, and through that to come to faith. For without faith one cannot receive God's grace, and without grace it is impossible to fulfill God's will.

Letter No. 9 to V. I. I.

You ask regarding sorrows in life: Are they necessary for man? This question is not stated correctly, though it does make some sense. The Lord created man for blessedness, and man truly was blessed until, through his sins, he corrupted all the good that the Lord had placed into his soul. Making of himself a god, to whom he directed all his goals and aspirations, he corrupted everything within and all that surrounded him. Every person is a god unto himself, and that is why there is such strife between people, such hatred toward one another. In order to be reborn, to return to our natural state, we must renounce the self, and our self-love, as Matushka Ardaliona taught. We must take our proper place, and our place is to yield to Him to whom alone belong true honor and worship. However, it is supremely difficult for a person to deny himself. He must die to his passions, and death is always hard and bitter. It is that much more difficult because those who surround him are all living in the same state of corruption as he is. They push each other toward perdition. Those who want to free themselves feel these shoves right in the face. Yet with the Lord's help and the renunciation of the passions, instead of pride He allows the soul to partake of humility; instead of self-love—love of neighbor; instead of hard-heartedness—compunction; instead of anger—meekness; instead of fear—faith; instead of despair—hope; instead of self-worship—love for God. Then sorrows begin to be a consolation in life. The soul rises above them; it does not feel them, but simply knows, sees, and feels the great assistance of God, strengthening the spirit in these sorrows and temptations of life. It comes to recognize the great wisdom of His path, which leads man to freedom through tribulations, and through these very tribulations cleanses the soul and leads it out of its wayward state, setting it on the right path. Then the soul experiences strength and joy and thanks God for the sorrows, which now appear to be insignificant compared to the benefits that He gives through sorrows.

LETTER NO. 10 TO V. I. I.

In your letter I see an expression which summarizes it all: "The demands of the soul and body arise from the laws of nature and follow these laws without regard to their sinfulness or holiness." Yes, this is so, and it shows us that man's nature is corrupt. Our spirit is so closely joined to our body that it constitutes one indivisible whole. If we develop our animal powers, we will become like beasts. By animal powers I mean not only physical, but all the powers of the soul given for earthly existence. If, on the other hand, we strive with God's help to develop the powers of the immortal spirit, this will certainly be to the detriment of our animal powers—it will even contradict all the laws and demands of our carnal nature. To rise above this nature is possible only for a soul that is strengthened by God's grace. You are right in saying that the laws of nature incline us to take actions akin to them, not discerning whether they are holy or sinful, not even asking for our agreement. This inclination of our animalistic self is termed natural within the fallen human state. Yet it is unnatural for our spirit, for through this it is persecuted, squelched, and destroyed. When we live according to the rules of our fallen nature, we sometimes feel an inexplicable melancholy, a lack of satisfaction, and an aspiration toward something higher, toward a freedom from all that comprises our earthly life. In this longing, in this desire for something more elevated, we should read the need of our spirit. If we suppress this voice within us, it will be altogether silenced or turn into a feeling of despair. Why is it so weak? Because as a consequence of the Fall, we cannot achieve any virtue by our own strength, and only God's grace can make us fruitful, when we give room for this grace through humility and faith. For this reason spiritual life is called supernatural. We must work on ourselves, and look for that which is loftier than earthly cares, and have faith that all things holy are brought about solely by God's grace—and this should make us humble.

Letter No. 11 to V. I. I.

Without justifying any deviation toward worldliness, I will neverthe-less tell you that, because you have a family and live in the world, it is impossible for you to devote yourself entirely to spiritual goals. You write that your activity is centered upon bodily pleasures, vainglory, and material security. You cannot divorce yourself from these pursuits, but even within this realm it is possible not to turn away from the path of salvation. If in following the demands of your fallen nature you under-take something for the sake of vainglory and you are successful, do not forget to thank the Lord for His mercy, to credit Him alone for this success, to accept from Him the satisfaction you have experienced, and to praise Him for the mercy which He has undeservedly granted you. If, on the other hand, you meet with failure and chagrin, and have to suffer dishonor instead of satisfaction, try to accept this from the Lord as something you deserve, humbling yourself before Him and request-ing even more humiliation for the sake of banishing your pride and self-love. Work on your heart so that it is able to forgive enemies, so that it does not act revengefully even in thought, but repays evil with good. You should act this way always and in all spheres of your activity. If something is done passionately, let every aspect of it be done according to God's word. Then you will see what to battle, and you will notice much weakness and powerlessness in your soul. It is then that faith will be rekindled in your heart. When God's help becomes apparent to you, you will be confirmed in your faith and hope in His power. It is not with the mind but with the heart that we must perceive both our own weakness and His strength.

Letter No. 12 to V. I. I.

Our Lord Jesus Christ took upon Himself human nature in order to cleanse it from the ancestral sin, and He died a shameful death on the cross in order to extinguish sin. Through the resurrection and ascension of our nature to Heaven, He gave us the power to become children of God. In baptism, we receive the promise of this adoption to sonship, and we can, if we desire, receive all the gifts of His grace. Through baptism, we entered the door that He Himself opened to us. If we travel on the path of His commandments, if we imitate His word and His example, if we become partakers of His kindness and truth, then the grace of Christ will be active within us, and not the ancestral sin. We must acquire faith in the Redeemer, faith in the fact that only through His righteousness can we be saved from our own unrighteousness. We are sanctified by His holiness, and His purity cleanses us of our filth. Without our Lord Jesus Christ, all of mankind was perishing in sins; without the Lord, each soul perishes in its own sin. Because we follow sinful inclinations and the will of our fallen nature, sin is rooted within us and has power over our soul, mind, and heart; it stands as a wall between us and the Lord. So we must cry out in prayer that He come to our soul and destroy this middle wall of enmity.[5]

Letter No. 13 to V. I. I.

You are justified in thinking that the condition I described to you is Christian perfection: when the heart is so expanded by love that no one and nothing can interfere with its dwelling in God's presence, with its being full of love for God and neighbor. Yes, this is perfection, and as with any perfection, it must stand before us as a goal at the end of a long journey. If we set this as a goal for ourselves, one which is distant but nevertheless desirable; if we strive to reach it and direct all of our feelings, thoughts, and deeds toward achieving this lofty goal; and if we use it to illumine our path, then we will see to what extent we willfully fall away from it or, with God's help, succeed in moving toward it. With such an understanding of the Christian life, I cannot advise you to do anything else but what I counseled earlier: to battle against your own passions. As to your relationship with your family member, here is my advice: do not be demanding of her, forgive her faults, be patient when your self-esteem is injured, and be self-sacrificing when you are compelled to endure various discomforts that proceed from the existing conflict within the family. If you are suffering greatly, if you have no strength to battle your passions and overcome them, give in to your weakness and let it humble you. Passions have such strength and power over us that, once we give in to them, we become their captives and they chain us, giving us no release. They blind our mind and do not allow us to see ourselves and our path clearly. Take care not to give way to your passions; better to devote yourself to the work of fulfilling God's commandments in order to be a servant of God.

Letter No. 14 to V. I. I.

How can you say that you are a ship without a rudder? Was it not today (January 6) that the Holy Church exclaimed to the faithful: "Christ is at hand, Who delivers the world from corruption." He is our anchor of salvation, the rudder that directs us toward the right path, the captain who steers our ship to the harbor of salvation—the Heavenly Kingdom. With Him all is well in our lives, with Him death is not frightening; with Him life after death is called eternal bliss. It is not a calamity that you did not achieve the rank of the priesthood as you wanted and that you are not a monk. You can leave those thoughts alone if this was not God's will: just never leave Christ. Let Him be the goal of all your endeavors, your heart's desire, your thoughts. Learn to love His will, His commandments; show some kindness to your neighbor for His sake, in word or deed. If you will love Christ, if for Him you oppose the sin-loving inclinations and desires of your heart, if you sacrifice for Him one of your minor passions, you will indeed be His priest, a secret monk, an angel. I read in the Patericon that once a layman and a monk were buried not far from one another. When later their coffins were opened, it was found that the layman was wearing a monk's habit, and the monk—laymen's clothing. You see, we do not know for sure who is a monk in the eyes of God. I consider you my spiritual son and desire to see you as a follower of Christ, as His disciple.

LETTER No. 15 TO V. I. I.

In order to preserve purity of the body, one must preserve purity of heart and mind. For this reason we need prayer, we need attentiveness toward our heart, and vigilant effort. If we are unable to constantly retain warmth of spiritual feeling—because it is a gift of God—we can at least constantly fortify our resolve to battle against the passions; we can enkindle within ourselves a striving toward perfection, and force ourselves to further spiritual endeavor. The commandments of God are not given to us arbitrarily, as though it is our choice whether or not to follow them. No, we are obligated to fulfill them, or else we will perish eternally. Thus I implore you: for God, for the fulfillment of His holy will, force yourself to bear the weaknesses of others, but to be strict and demanding toward yourself. It would be good for you to occasionally read the lives of saints and to have at least a short but consistent prayer rule. In order to begin paying attention to your heart, here is what I advise you to do during this lent. Some time ago I suggested that you learn by heart the prayer of St John Chrysostom: "O Lord, deprive me not of Thy heavenly good things." Now I advise you, beginning with the first prayer, to retain one of these prayers within your mind and to repeat it as often as possible through the course of the day. Today, use the first one: "O Lord, deprive me not . . . " Tomorrow, the second one: "O Lord, deliver me from the eternal torments . . . " Carry this prayer in your mind, heart, and imagination. When you ask for heavenly good things, contrast them with earthly good things. Allow your heart to feel all the futility of these earthly good things, their transience, their inconstancy. Consider each petition in this way. Let your soul dwell on these prayers throughout the day. If good thoughts come as a result of this, write them down; if you experience contrition, guard it through solitude. Feed your soul, occupy your mind, direct your imagination. May your humble efforts bear fruit, that you not hunger eternally in the life to come.

Letter No. 16 to V. I. I.

I judge no one, for I myself am sinful. Yet all of us are judged by the word of God, which is given to us for the governing of our lives, for our salvation and purification, to show us the path to eternal life. It judges us when we ignore it, when we transgress it. And it will judge us in the life to come as well. It is fearful to sin against it. It is fearful because the heart grows hardened and the word of God no longer penetrates it. This condition is worse than physical death. Do not trifle with feelings. Like fire, they can destroy everything that has been instilled in the soul, heart, and mind. They will burn everything that has been implanted by the word of God, leaving the soul alone with its passions and sins. One must preserve purity of both body and soul; otherwise, the soul will perish eternally. This death is more dreadful than anything that exists either in heaven or on earth. Take a look at the lives of saints, how the righteous ones sought the Lord with all their strength.

Letter No. 17 to V. I. I.

We should never give in to our passions, even in small ways. One prosecutes a thief even when he steals because he has nothing to eat. Even this natural need does not excuse the theft. Be strict with yourself. Every indulgence of one's passions destroys the purity of moral perception. The conscience, the natural moral law written on our hearts, becomes deaf if we ignore its promptings, if we act contrary to its precepts. Do I want this or not? is not an appropriate question here. This is irrelevant in terms of the moral law of the salvation of the soul.

Instead of one's own desires, there must be God's commandment, the will of God, which leads to eternal life. If you were at war, could you say, "I do not want to engage in battle"? No, you would go, without thinking, you would go even if you were sure to die. So it is in spiritual battle: if God's commandments require a struggle, how can we say that we do not want to fight, that it is more agreeable to give ourselves up to our enemies? How shameful! How dreadful it is in this life when one's will is weakened to such a state. And in the future life, the soul will endure even more shame, when all of its deeds and thoughts are revealed. One must ask and entreat the Lord to strengthen our will against passionate thoughts; to turn our strength, all our strivings, and our heart's desires to higher goals: holy, lofty, and noble. I will pray that the Lord give you the determination not only to endure and to suffer, but even to die for His commandments.

Letter No. 18 to V. I. I.

When the conscience and heart are pure before God, He prevents our going astray. If we wander off course through our own sinfulness, we will not see the will of God in our actions. May God grant you to be a good Christian, constantly keeping before you the Lord and His holy will, not your own pleasures, nor the gratification of your passions and sensual desires. You tell me that besides all the attractiveness of sinful desires and all manner of entertainments, there lives in your soul a striving toward spiritual life, which sometimes makes itself felt very strongly—even during the amusements themselves. Do you realize that such a striving of the soul is God's call? Do not extinguish this enlivening feeling, but preserve it. A flame cannot burn in a wind; it will be extinguished. Similarly, God's grace beckons us, but the wind of passions and diversions extinguishes the light and warmth of the Divine fire. Persist in prayer and the reading of the word.

Letter No. 19 to V. I. I.

The Lord saves us in multiple ways. Those difficult physical ailments that often visit you constantly remind you of death. But what can be more beneficial for the soul than the remembrance of death? It frees us from all earthly attachments; it reveals to us the actual worth of earthly deeds. Most of all, it helps us to strive toward eternal life. May God grant that your illnesses bear fruit for your soul—salvation. We believe that everything that the Lord arranges serves for our benefit and eternal salvation.

The current set of letters is written to a certain person identified only as M. S.

Letter No. 1 to M. S.

I thank you for your feelings of love and devotion which you expressed in your letter and in your poetry sent on the 6th of the month. I know that you have always loved to listen to my words, the word of God, the word of salvation, which I have shared. It always uplifts your spirit and even strengthens you physically. In this I see your love for God, the desire to follow His word, and your devotion toward me. Now that you are ill and somewhat despondent, I regret that I cannot see you and speak with you in person. I want to tell you not to lose heart, not to be dispirited. When I was your age I had a similar illness; my nerves were frayed to the limit, and my head was reeling from faintness and weakness, to the point that I sometimes lost consciousness . . . I also expected to lose my sanity; even the doctors predicted something of that sort. Thanks be to God, this did not happen, and in time my nerves became stronger. With strength of soul, the Lord sends physical endurance as well.

This is not what I wish to tell you, however. It's more important to convey to you how I viewed my condition at the time, how I dealt with it. Thinking that I was dying, I entrusted my fate, both temporal and eternal, into the hands of God. I wanted His will to be manifested in my life. I wanted all my desires and endeavors to be directed solely toward obedience to His holy will and submission to His Providence. When I thought that I would lose my sanity I agreed to this without murmuring, without fear, as my condition allowed me to see the utter poverty of human nature. I was ready to do without the powers of the soul, without health for the body, without reason or a mind—if only my spirit was not contrary to the will of God, that it was humbled before Him. To Him alone I gave glory, honor, and worship. In this state my soul rejoiced; it rejoiced that He alone is great, wise, and mighty. May the Lord grant that this joy of salvation in the One God, this faith in Him, and devotion to His will be in your heart also. May God preserve you through His grace.

Letter No. 2 to M. S.

. . . Why do you feel a morbid and oppressive sensation in your heart? What is this from? Certainly, this is because of passions. *"Where the Spirit of the Lord is, there is liberty."*[6] And I say, where there is passion, there is straitness and suffering. The fact that passions live in our hearts is indisputable, but if we are not conscious of them and act according to their dictates, they do not torment us. Nor do they torment us when, being conscious of them, we war against them. But when we are conscious of them in ourselves and do not want to stand up against them with all the powers of our soul; when with one part of our soul we repudiate them but with the other we give ear to their sweet utterances; when we avoid exposing them; when we lack the resolve to walk the path of the Cross behind our Teacher, the Cross-bearer—then, of course, we will feel oppression and pain. The Lord, who took upon Himself all of our sins and frailties, showed us an example of this battle of the will. In the Garden of Gethsemane He felt tormented until His will agreed to accept suffering. Try your heart and you will see that there are many contradictions in it. One must, once and for all, commit one's soul to being guided by God's will to the fulfillment of His commandments, and to the rigorous rules of monastic life. When the soul agrees with this, all will become easier.

I admire your ability to engage yourself and to be inspired with all that is holy and good, but do not forget that the self-denial that lies at the foundation of monasticism is better and higher than anything else. "Run from people and you will be saved." Run from everything into the depth of your own heart, in order to be with the only One. May the Lord preserve you. I pray to Him for you and entrust you to Him.

LETTER NO. 3 TO M. S.

. . . May the Lord God help you! He will fortify your spirit. For my part, I will share with you a word of experience. In any confusion and temptation the only solution and return to peacefulness is humility. It is only by following this path that the soul comes to the truth that resolves everything to warmth, which heals, and to freedom, which assuages any disturbance of the soul. If you lose this path, your soul will be surrounded by darkness and oppression, and it will arrive at faulty reasoning. This is disastrous, for faulty reasoning shows everything in a distorted way. All of the circumstances of life appear bitter and treacherous; one does not see in them the paths of God, His salutary Providence. Men seem not like brothers but enemies, and their faults are grossly magnified. Our own frailties become frightening and even present themselves as active manifestations of inner sufferings. Yes, only one path can save in such cases— the path of humility. Read Psalm 50 three times a day. Read it, forcing yourself, even during the Cherubic Hymn in church, and the Lord will open to you the meaning of true repentance and humility of spirit.

The current set of letters is written to a certain person identified only as A. S.

LETTER NO. 1 TO A. S.

I am glad that your visit to the monastery brought you comfort. It is a great mercy of God when there is a place on earth where the soul can find delight, when there are people with whom our heart can rest. But why do you attribute all this to me? Without the Lord we cannot receive anything, nor can we give anything without Him. He gives us everything through His grace. Those who loved Him saw Him everywhere and in all things. And He revealed to them His living word, His will, and the paths of His providence. How did He do this? Through the purity of their hearts. With God's help, we must guard our hearts from passions. Most important of all, we need to guard against doubts and pride, against falsehood and self-justification, against lack of love and contempt for our neighbor. If, by God's grace, we are able to prevent these passions from ruling our heart, we will be capable of embracing the counsels of God's word, of following His will. I rejoice with you, my dear, that your heart is open to God's word. May the Lord grant that it also be open to fulfilling His will. Pray fervently to the Mother of God that She show you the way of God's providence; for on any path, those who fear the Lord will find Him by way of His commandments, by laboring and struggling against the evil and vice which live within us. May God give you the strength not to turn aside from this path, no matter where you might live!

LETTER NO. 2 TO A. S.

With the Lord, I fear nothing. I walk my way and before me I see or desire to see only my goal—no matter what it is—the one I am striving toward. I am intent on that goal and I see nothing else, nor have I any desire to see anything else. Herein is power. No intrigue can withstand such power; it will not even touch it. *"The Lord is my helper, and I will not fear what man shall do unto me."*[7]

Letter No. 3 to A. S.

I believe you that your life is not easy. Your parents are sick and nothing is being done as you would like; all this causes you suffering. Yet why does the disciple of Christ tell us to be thankful for everything? He says: *"Pray without ceasing, in everything give thanks."*[8] For everything—that means for all the sorrows and for everything unpleasant that happens in life. Yes, first one needs to strengthen one's faith that everything occurs according to God's will. One needs to agree to submit to this Holy will. One needs to humble the heart, to consider oneself unworthy of better circumstances. Only then can one be thankful for everything. Bishop Ignatius taught his disciples to frequently repeat the following prayer in times of grievous circumstances and in times of joy: "Glory be to God for all things!" And again, "Glory be to God for all things!" With this prayer all rancor leaves the heart, confusion disappears, and such peace and joy enter the soul. . . . The Lord has light that dispels all confusion. One needs only to approach Him with faith!

[Letter Number 4 was of a personal nature and is not included here.]

Letter No. 5 to A. S.

I was hoping to see you in person and speak to you directly. I left several letters from you unanswered because I found them difficult to reply to by mail. Your letters are so good, and I read them with joy. I hear in them a living soul that feels deeply and possesses a keen spiritual intuition. I also see a fine, well-developed mind, which understands and sees itself and all that goes on within the soul so clearly. I thank God for you. I am gladdened and consoled by you. What's more, your heart is ready to live for others and to give them everything. But do not become proud on hearing this praise, for now I need to reproach you as well.

I must reproach you for your exaggerated self-abasement, for demanding perfection of yourself. Only the Lord is perfect and all holy. We mortals all have weaknesses and flaws. And how good it is that we can attain perfection only in Him and through Him! If we believe that He is almighty, then we must also believe that He can do everything for our benefit—if this is according to His holy will. If we believe that He is all good, all generous, then we must trust that He will give us all that is needful. If we believe that He is omniscient, we must rely entirely upon His will, and believe in the righteousness of His judgments, His providence. He is able to give us everything, and He desires to give us all that is good. If He does not give us what we want, what we think would be beneficial and good, even that which would serve for our salvation, it means that either we are not ready to accept this, or the time for this has not come, and the gift would bring us harm if it were given according to our wishes.

You have flaws that you have difficulty in battling at times; you ask for God's help and do not feel His help. But you have not applied sufficient effort, and this effort in itself is essential, just as it is essential for us to see our own powerlessness, so that in this struggle our will, our resolve, might be strengthened. Most important, the soul needs to realize its utter weakness and to humble itself profoundly, casting all of its hope upon the One Lord who saves us all. The Holy Fathers, in teaching us to battle with the passions, counseled: "Fall and get up." This does not mean to fall in the sense of committing a sin or entertaining a sinful feeling, but fall through the weakening of the will, of resolve to fight the sinful thought. And then rise again, that is, strengthen your resolve, resume your struggle against sin. One who falls cannot immediately jump up and run. He is hurt, all of his limbs are sore, he has barely recovered after the fall, and he will be weak in battle until he gathers his strength or until someone comes to his help. So it is with our will. If it falls, that is, if it entertains a sinful thought, it becomes weak, broken, powerless. In this debilitated state it must get up and begin to fight anew, even though it is injured and half dead. It must call upon Him Who alone can help—but even its voice has no strength, it has become mute. But when help comes from the grace of God, our resolve will be strengthened and arise again.

LETTER NO. 6 TO A. S.

I have not written since leaving St Petersburg, but I often, very often, converse with you in my thoughts. My stay in St Petersburg was like a dream, a good dream. Our trip to Kronstadt to see Fr John, his visit to our home, everything he said—this all seems like time spent in another world, a perfect, holy world. Now I have understood the meaning of all he said to me—not only with my soul, but through the experience of life itself. All that happened to me was exactly as he predicted, and his word supported me, directed my spirit, gave it purpose, and even the experience itself bore fruit. By God's allowance, a multitude of adversities came upon me, just as he had said. But do not worry! By God's mercy, granted me through the prayers of Fr John, all is now passing, just as if a storm were subsiding, and both the sorrows and temptations have passed.

LETTER No. 7 TO A. S.

Is it pleasing to the Lord to grant our request for peace and tranquility of life? We do not dare to demand something even of another person, let alone ask and expect God to fulfill our request. We do not even know what is beneficial for us and what is harmful. Yet we can see God's help, His mercy toward us, in that He enables us to endure the unbearable with patience, humility, and submission to His holy will. This is a great mercy of God—and I see it acting in your case. You are able to endure that which human strength alone cannot. You endure this with humility and submissiveness. Your heart does not become hardened against your offender. Is it not God's help that works with you and strengthens your spirit? Only trust in the Lord and give everything over to Him. By ways known to Him alone He will draw everyone to Himself, to peace and salvation. Let us pray to Him, then, that His holy will be accomplished in us.

LETTER No. 8 TO A. S.

What does it mean to believe in God? One must believe not only in the existence of God the Creator and in salvation given to us through Jesus Christ, but one must also believe steadfastly—in all of life's circumstances, not matter how difficult—that God is merciful, that He desires our salvation, and that, seeing and knowing what is beneficial for us not only temporally but also eternally, He leads us in that direction as a loving, wise father would his own children, with an even-handed love, kindness, and strictness. For this reason, we must accept everything with trust in God's mercy, asking only for His help in all trials and temptations, whether they come from our own weakness or from people, who are tools of God which He employs for our salvation—and often for their benefit as well. Through our humility, our close ones who offend us can also be brought to salvation.

The current set of letters is written to a certain person identified only as V. P. G.

Letter No. 1 to V. P. G.

You ask whether or not your mother sees you. Doubtless she does, but not in the way that we earthly ones see; nor does she feel as we earthly ones feel. She has no egoism, self-love, desire for personal earthly happiness and satisfaction. Her soul lives in and for God as the One Source of Life. It is from this perspective that she sees your soul—whether or not your thoughts, feelings, and desires are pleasing to God. It would gladden her to see you doing God's will and fulfilling His commandments in relation to Him and your neighbor while you live on this earth. Do not regret that sometimes you grieved her. Be assured that she has forgotten all about this and has forgiven you. Now, with her bodiless soul, she understands that all earthly tribulations, great and small, were but tools for the purification of [her] soul, and she has glorified and thanked the Lord for everything, for He provides all for the salvation of the soul. So, my dear, put aside your sorrow and oppressive remorse. Instead, firmly resolve to benefit from this experience before her immortal soul and in future try to act not according to your whims or passions, but according to God's commandments and the needs of those whom the Lord places on your life's path. Your mother will see you acting thus and will rejoice at your kind works and intentions.

Letter No. 2 to V. P. G.

The dignity and nobility of a person depend not so much upon the advantages received through his ancestors, but upon his own merits and the virtues acquired through his effort in battling vice within his heart. This is what the Lord values in us, and wise people do likewise. A person should value all that is given to him by the Lord. The Lord has given you so much, my dear, that you should be not despondent but grateful to Him.

Now let us speak of another matter. The Holy Fathers always advise that we not make any decision while our soul is troubled. In this state we are unable to discern properly, let alone perceive, God's will with a clear conscience and a peaceful heart. For when the heart and spirit are confused, the Sun of Righteousness is hidden from the soul's view. It is wiser to wait with this decision, not to hurry, and for the time being not to speak of it to anyone. Monastic life is very difficult. It requires a special calling from God, a certain deeply felt need to live by the loftiest of ideals. Without such a calling it doesn't even make any sense.

Letter No. 3 to V. P. G.

You worry so much, my dear, because you have little faith in God. After all, without His will not even one hair will fall from our heads. Give everything over to Him. Grow to love His will, desire that all happens in accordance with it, and calm your heart with such faith. I wish you health, entreat you to undergo treatment seriously, and to live under God's guidance.

Letter No. 4 to V. P. G.

When you are assailed by your impatience, remember how much and how long prisoners endure solitary confinement, whereas you are not in prison but surrounded by comfort and the company of others. You must take yourself in hand; assign yourself a prayer rule and make it a practice to tolerate deprivation, loneliness. This is necessary for a monastic in order to come to God with a patient heart, solitary and passionless. You must make a beginning.

Letter No. 5 to V. P. G.

The Lord is constantly sending you heavy crosses to bear. It appears to me that this is His holy will, and that you are being tested in order to learn patience and self-denial. You say that you are far from possessing a pure heart. Every person is far from any true virtue, particularly spiritual goodness and purity of heart. Without God, without His help and grace, a person cannot even come close to the concept of true spiritual virtue. So the Lord Himself is leading you, is training your inner self, leading it to purification and wisdom, sending afflictions and labors in order to train you to be patient, to be obedient to God's will, and to acknowledge your own weakness. What is a person to do? Just one thing—submit to the Lord's will and cry out to Him in humility of spirit: "Lead me Thyself, O Lord, whither Thou knowest, and help me to fulfill Thy will." And how easy it is, how salvific, to walk the path that is indicated by the Lord. May the Lord help you be obedient to Him in all things!

Letter No. 6 to V. P. G.

It saddens me to think of how upset you were yesterday. Are you ill, perhaps? If you are distressed by the thought that I will no longer be an abbess, let me assure you that this is not so. I tell you honestly that I always strive to do everything according to God's will. I have my own desires, and I will express them, but in my soul there is one thought, one desire: that all be done according to God's will. And in this case, even if I wish to spend my final years in solitude, this is not my decision but only a desire. And my desire is that everything that happens in my life be according to God's will. With this foundation in my soul, this dedication to God's will, my heart is peaceful and never upset or dissatisfied when things do not go the way I desired or expected. I advise you to seek such spiritual peace within your own heart, leaving all to God's will, and to learn to love it and to do your utmost to submit to it. One Holy Father said, "If the heavens were to collide with the earth, even then I would not be afraid." May God grant that you, too, firmly resolve to dedicate yourself to the fulfillment of His holy will.

ACKNOWLEDGMENTS

Holy Trinity Publications wishes to thank the editorial staff of the journal *Orthodox Life* who discovered this vital work of the spiritual heritage of Russian Orthodoxy and first prepared the letters for print. We would like to thank Mary Mansur for her scrupulous proofreading of every letter in this translation. In addition, we are grateful to Nikodemos Press for providing Holy Trinity Publications the opportunity to publish this work. May this book offer edification and encouragement for those striving to live the Christian life.

END NOTES

Introduction

   1. Igumenia Arsenia, *Zhizneopisanie, Pis'ma k P.A. Brianchaninovu I drugim litsam* (Moskovskoye Podvor'e Sviato-Troitskoi Sergievoi Lavri, 1998), 52–53.

   2. Arsenia, *Zhizneopisanie*, 25.

   3. Arsenia, *Zhizneopisanie*, 227–228.

   4. St Ignatius (1807–1867), well known for his ascetic writings such as *The Arena*, was glorified by the Russian Church in 1988. He is commemorated on April 30.

   5. Matt 16:24.

A Short Biography

   1. The Ust'-Medveditskii Monastery, originally built in 1652 with the blessing of Patriarch Joachim, was closed and desecrated after the Russian Revolution. More than fifty buildings on the territory of the monastery were destroyed. Efforts to rebuild it began in 1992, when the diocese of Volgograd reopened it as a male monastery. Since 2001 it has once again been functioning as a convent.

   2. Gennady Chebotarev, dir., *Igumenia Arsenia [Sebriakova]* (Volgograd, 2007), accessed April 24, 2015, from www.youtube.com/watch?v=YgWfMFhzNZY. This documentary film was compiled by the parish of the Urupinskaya icon of the Mother of God.

   3. Chebotarev, *Igumenia Arsenia*.

   4. Arsenia, *Zhizneopisanie*, 71.

Abbess Arsenia actually did the digging herself, with the help of several nuns who were closest to her. These caves survive to this day. They contain a holy item—a special rock slab that contains the imprints of the hands and knees of the Mother of God. According to the monastery tradition, Abbess Arsenia saw a vision: the Mother of God praying upon this rock. The monastery catalogs the many healings that have taken place at this site.

Part I: The Notes of Abbess Arsenia

1. Gen 3:18.
2. Gen 3:19.
3. Gen 3:19.
4. John 6:54.
5. John 7:38.
6. Gen 3:19.
7. Ps 45:11.

Part II: The Letters to Peter Alexandrovich Brianchaninov

1. This is a reference to the *Ascetic Works of St Ignatius Brianchaninov*—Ed.
2. Added by translator for clarification—Ed.
3. Clarification mine—Ed.
4. John 15:3.
5. Gen 3:19.
6. Rom 8:39.
7. Ps 138:8.
8. Paraphrase of Gen. 3:19.
9. Luke 17:21.
10. Josh 23:23.
11. Matt 3:3.
12. Jas 1:20.
13. Jas 1:15.
14. 1 Tim 1:15.
15. Letter No. 77 is from 2012 OL—Ed.
16. St Tikhon of Zadonsk—Ed.

Part III: Letters to Other Individuals

1. Ps 15:3.
2. 1 Cor 12:3.
3. Cf. Luke 11:39: *"make the outside of the cup and dish clean, but your inward part is full of greed and wickedness."*

4. Cf. Mark 7:21–22: "*For from within, out of the heart of men, proceed evil thoughts, adulteries, fornications, murders, thefts, covetousness, wickedness, deceit, lewdness, an evil eye, blasphemy, pride, foolishness.*"

5. Cf. Eph 2:14–15: "*For He Himself is our peace, who has made both one, and has broken down the middle wall of separation, having abolished in His flesh the enmity, that is, the law of commandments contained in ordinances, so as to create in Himself one new man from the two, thus making peace.*"

6. 2 Cor 3:17.

7. Ps 117:6.

8. 1 Thess 5:17–18.

INDEX

New Year, 26, 46
Nikolo-Babaevskii Monastery, ix, xii

obedience, 33, 39, 42, 58, 66, 82, 90
omniscience, 86
oppression, 32, 82–83, 88
Optina Monastery, 55
Osipov, Professor Alexei, ix

Pafnutia, Schema-nun, 10, 57, 64–65
pain, 10, 12, 83
paradise, 27, 67
Pascha, vii, 28, 33, 36
passions, vii, viii, 1–3, 10, 24, 27, 29–30,
    33, 41–42, 46, 50, 55, 69–71, 74–75,
    78–80, 82–84
path(s), 15–16, 22, 25, 28, 31, 38, 42–43,
    61, 65–66, 71, 74–75, 83–84
patience, 18, 33, 37, 42–43, 50, 87, 90
peace, 1, 11, 17–18, 32, 46, 87
    inner, 51
    prayer in, 36, 50–51
    of soul, 50, 60
    spiritual, 50
perdition, 16, 46, 64, 67, 74–75
perfection, 63, 77, 79, 85–86
persecution, 5, 76
Peter of Damascus, 30
Petersburg, 27, 44, 86
Philokalia, The, 57
podvig, 15, 37
Polovtsev, Archimandrite Juvenal, 55
possessions, 43
poverty, 26
    spiritual, 41, 43, 72
powerlessness, 53, 72–73, 77, 86
praise, 20, 26, 30, 39
prayer, 1–2, 13, 17, 24–25, 35, 85, 87
    attention to, 12
    common, 28
    compelling to, 50

of faith, 35
fervent, 84
Jesus, 5, 12, 52–53, 55
Lord's, 37, 47
for neighbor, 51
in peace, 36, 50–51
pure, 3, 35
soul and, 53
spirit of, 53
spiritual, 1
thoughts during, 11
prejudice, 33
pride, 5, 57, 70, 76
priesthood, 67, 78
prophets, 43, 66
Providence, 12, 46, 83–84, 86
Psalter, xi, 53
punishment, 5–6
purification, 80, 90
purity, 1, 7, 17, 80

Redeemer, 19, 60, 77
rejoice, 49, 88
remembrance of death 34, 44, 81
remembrance of God, 1, 32
renunciation, 3, 12, 25, 40, 43, 60, 73, 75
repentance, 13, 15, 41, 53–56, 58, 61,
    67, 73
respite, 56, 58
rest, 56, 60
resurrection, 26, 49, 77
righteousness, 22, 37–39, 45, 56, 60–61,
    86, 89

saints, vii, 47, 60, 66, 68
salvation, viii–ix, 4, 10–12, 15–18,
    20–21, 23–25, 30, 34, 37, 41, 44,
    46–47, 56, 59, 61, 64, 67, 72, 74, 76,
    80–82, 86–88
sanctification, 17, 60, 68
sanity, 82